Dimensions of Sight Singing

LONGMAN MUSIC SERIES
Series Editor: Gerald Warfield

Dimensions
of
Sight Singing

An Anthology

Paul Cooper

The Shepherd School of Music
Rice University

Longman
New York & London

Dimensions of Sight Singing
An Anthology

Longman, Inc., 19 West 44th St., New York, N.Y. 10028
Associated companies, branches, and representatives
throughout the world.

Developmental Editor: Gordon T. R. Anderson
Editorial and Design Supervisor: Joan Matthews
Interior Design: George Chien
Cover Design: Charles C. Fellows
Manufacturing and Production Supervisor: Maria Chiarino
Composition: A&S Graphics
Printing and Binding: Murray Printing Company

Library of Congress Cataloging in Publication Data

Main entry under title:

Dimensions of sight singing.

  (Longman music series)
  Bibliography: p.
  Includes index.
  1. Sight-singing. I. Cooper, Paul. II. Series.
MT870.M87   784.9'4   79-22146
ISBN: 0-582-28159-8

Manufactured in the United States of America

9 8 7 6 5 4 3 2 1

To NADIA BOULANGER
with admiration and affection

who, through her profound insights
into the great music of all eras,
has inspired three generations
to seek out the miracles
of the Muses' art.

Contents

Foreword by Elmer Thomas   *xiii*
Acknowledgments   xv
Introduction   xvii
Organization and Purpose   xix
A Note of Explanation to Students and Teachers   xxi

Part One.   How to Learn to Sight-Sing

1. Early Sacred Chant   3
2. *Organum*; Polyphony through the *Ars Antiqua*   16
3. Secular Songs from the Eleventh to Fourteenth Centuries   25
4. Sacred and Secular Music from the Fourteenth and Fifteenth Centuries   39
5. Sacred and Secular Music from the ''Golden Age of Polyphony''   55
6. Diverse Examples from the Seventeenth Century   79
7. Vocal Music of the Late Baroque Period   98
8. Mostly Canons: Haydn, Mozart, Beethoven, and Schubert   124
9. Songs and Operatic Excerpts from the Nineteenth Century   151
10. Vocal Music from the Twentieth Century: 1900–1950   190
11. Music since 1950   224

Part Two.   Folk Songs

12. Folk Songs in Major Key   243
13. Folk Songs in Minor Key   262
14. Folk Songs Using Modal Resources   270
15. Folk Songs Employing Mixed Modes   280

Appendix.   Language Pronunciation Guides: Latin, French, German, Italian   292

Musical Examples

BASIC

8A–B	*Aeterna Christi munera*, Gregorian chant	12
1	*Aeterne rerum conditor*, Ambrosian chant	6
35	*Angelica biltà*, Francesco Landini	42
145	*As I was going to Banbury*, folk song	251
49	*Aus tiefer Not*, Johann Walter	63
14	*Benedicamus Domino*, melismatic organum	18
157	*Birchbark song, the*, folk song	262
23	*C'est la fin*, Guillaume d'Amiens	27
33	*Comment qu'a moy*, Guillaume de Machaut	41
135	*Cool, sweet water, the*, folk song	244
142	*Crocodile song*, folk song	249
118	*Der Mai tritt ein mit Freuden*, Arnold Schönberg	195
6A–B	*Deus, miserere*, Gregorian chant	11
42	*Dew, a dew, a*, Robert Cornysh	57
25	*En mà dame*, Perrin d'Agincourt	29
98	*Entflieh' mit mir*, Felix Mendelssohn	152
86A–D	*Erstes Gebot*, Franz Joseph Haydn	129–130
99	*Es fiel ein Reif*, Felix Mendelssohn	153
46	*Et incarnatus est*, Josquin des Prez	60
61	*Exultent caeli*, Claudio Monteverdi	85
138	*Fare ye well*, folk song	246
131	*Forbidden fruit*, Gerald Warfield	232
65	*Gleich wie ein kleines Vögelein*, Johann Hermann Schein	92
137	*Good-bye brother*, folk song	245
148	*Hark! the cock crows*, folk song	253
82	*Herr von Gänsewitz zu seinem Kammerdiener*, Franz Joseph Haydn	126
9A–B	*Heu, pius pastor*, Gregorian chant	13
96	*Introit*, Franz Schubert	143
44	*Isbruck, ich muss dich lassen*, Heinrich Isaac	58
140	*I want to go home*, folk song	247
3A–B	*Kyrie eleison*, Gallican chant	9
167	*Little partridge*, folk song	271
127	*Love is a circle*, Ross Lee Finney	225
168	*Lullaby*, folk song	272
29A–B	*Mayenzeit one neidt*, Neidhart von Reuental	34–35
4	Modes, the medieval church	10
10A–B	*Mulier, quid ploras?* Gregorian chant	13
15	*Nobilis, humilis, Magne*, organum in thirds	18
139	*No more rain for wet you*, folk song	247
144	*O now this glorious Eastertide*, folk song	250
143	*On, roll on, my ball roll on*, folk song	250
24	*Or la truix*, trouvère song	27
21	*O Roma nobilis*, goliard	26
170	*Peter Gray*, folk song	274
159	*Prisoner, the*, folk song	264
48	*Quando ritrova*, Costanzo Festa	62
26	*Quand voi en la fin*, Perrin d'Agincourt	29
12	*Rex caeli, domine*, parallel organum	17
158	*Sigurd and Hamling*, folk song	263

13　　*Sit gloria Domini,* organum at the fifth　　17

85　　*Thy voice o harmony,* Franz Joseph Haydn　　125

80　　*Tod und Schlaf,* Franz Joseph Haydn　　125

166　　*Two maidens, the,* folk song　　270

5　　*Ut queant laxis,* Guido d'Arezzo　　10

64　　*Viel schöner Blümelein,* Johann Hermann Schein　　92

81　　*Vixi,* Franz Joseph Haydn　　125

22　　*Vos n'aler,* Guillaume d'Amiens　　26

58　　*What if I never speed,* John Dowland　　76

28　　*Willekommen Mayenshein,* Neidhart von Reuental　　33

MODERATE

40　　*Adieu m'amour et ma maistresse,* Gilles Binchois　　50

66　　*Ah! Ah! Ah! My Anne,* Henry Purcell (to be prepared)　　93

51　　*Ainsi qu'on oit le cerf bruire,* Claude Goudimel　　66

160　　*All on the grass,* folk song　　264

95　　*An den Tod,* Franz Schubert　　141

57　　*Ardo per mio destin,* Cosimodi Bottegari　　75

178　　*Arirang,* folk song　　281

105　　*Auf ein altes Bild,* Hugo Wolf　　170

45　　*Ave Maria,* Heinrich Isaac　　59

176　　*Ay la le lo,* folk song　　278

37　　*Beata mater,* John Dunstable (to be prepared)　　44

17　　*Beata viscera,* perotin　　19

16　　*Benedicamis Domino,* melismatic organum　　19

97　　*Benediction,* Franz Schubert　　146

53　　*Benedictus,* Giovanni Palestrina　　68

151　　*Boat-haulers' song,* folk song　　256

56　　*Cantai un tempo,* Cosimo di Bottegari　　74

180　　*Children do linger,* folk song　　282

120　　*Chanson du clair tamis,* Frances Poulenc　　199

70　　*Christ lag in Todesbanden,* Johann Sebastian Bach　　101

141　　*Cocks are a-crowing,* folk song　　248

174　　*Cuckoo, the,* folk song　　277

111　　*Dissonance, a,* Alexander Borodin　　179

59　　*Dovrò dunque morire,* Giulio Caccini (to be prepared)　　81

181　　*Down the mountain,* folk song　　283

161　　*Down the street,* folk song　　265

129　　*Dreaming of a dead lady,* Lennox Berkeley　　228

94　　*Dreifach ist der Schritt der Zeit,* Franz Schubert　　139

100　　*Du bist wie eine Blume,* Robert Schumann　　154

73　　*Ein' feste Burg ist unser Gott,* Johann Sebastian Bach　　103

182　　*Exile, the,* folk song　　284

146　　*Fivelgöer Christmas carol,* folk song　　252

163　　*For a kiss,* folk song　　267

123　　*Fortune plango vulnera,* Carl Orff　　210

36　　*Gloria in excelsis,* Worcester school　　43

90　　*Glück zum neuen Jahr,* Ludwig van Beethoven　　136

93　　*Gold'ner Schein,* Franz Schubert　　138

107　　*Göttlicher Morpheus,* Johannes Brahms　　107

84　　*Grabschrift,* Franz Joseph Haydn　　128

152　　*Groyle Machree,* folk song　　256

179　　*Hallelu, hallelu,* folk song　　282

68	*Hark, Harry*, John Eccles	96
76–77	*Heroes, when with glory burning*, George Frederick Handel (to be prepared)	112
155	*Honey-ant song of Ljába*, folk song	259
89	*Ich bitt' dich*, Ludwig van Beethoven	134
101	*Ich grolle nicht*, Robert Schumann	155
106	*Ich schwing mein Horn*, Johannes Brahms	172
31	*Ich setze*, Walther von der Vogelweide	36
67	*I gave her cakes*, Henry Purcell	96
43	*I have been a foster*, Robert Cooper	57
50	*In manus tuas, Domine*, Thomas Tallis	64
7A–B	*Insignis praeconiis*, Gregorian chant	11–12
183	*In the garden a beggar there was*, folk song	285
74	*Jesu, meine Freude*, Johann Sebastian Bach	104
171	*Katie Kádár*, folk song	274
156	*Keel row*, folk song	260
185	*Keys of the jail, the*, folk song	287
150	*Kiss ye the baby*, folk song	255
11	*Kyrie eleison*, Gregorian chant	14
27	*Le jeu de Robin et Marion*, Adam de la Halle	30
173	*Lord Gregory*, folk song	276
112	*Lydia*, Gabriel Fauré	181
128	*Lyke-wake dirge, a*, Igor Stravinsky	226
175	*Maiden of the dark brown hair*, folk song	278
169	*Maid of Newfoundland, the*, folk song	273
18	*Mira lege, mira modo*, twelfth century hymn	20
104	*Mit einer Primulaveris*, Edvard Grieg	167
110	*Morgen*, Richard Strauss	176
19	*Nato nobis hodie*, thirteenth century hymn	21
162	*Negev desert dance*, folk song	266
149	*No other moon*, folk song	254
30	*Nû al'erst*, Walther von der Vogelweide	36
188	*O dance, you maids*, folk song	290
20	*O mitissima*, thirteenth century motet (to be prepared)	22
165	*O ola, ola*, folk song	269
136	*Overlander, the*, folk song	244
61	*Perche se m'odiavi*, Claudio Monteverdi (to be prepared)	84
47	*Pleni sunt coeli*, Josquin des Pres	61
172	*Ploughing song*, folk song	275
34	*Plus dure*, Machaut (to be prepared)	44
69	*Qui tollis*, Johann Joseph Fux	100
41	*Sanctus*, Johannes Ockeghem	52
102	*Schmerzen*, Richard Wagner	158
62	*Scorto da te*, Claudio Monteverdi	88
147	*Sea chantey*, folk song	252
154	*Shepherds, hark!* folk song	258
91	*Si non per portas*, Ludwig van Beethoven	137
109	*Spruch*, Johannes Brahms	175
32	*Sumer is icumen in*, c. 1310	37
153	*Twelve lads*, folk song	258
71	*Valet will ich dir geben*, Johann Sebastian Bach	102
83	*Vergebliches Glück*, Franz Joseph Haydn	127
2A–B	*Victimae paschali laudes*, 11th century	6–8
164	*Vito, the*, folk song	268
72	*Vom Himmel hoch, da komm' ich her*, Johann Sebastian Bach	102

108   *Wann?* Johannes Brahms   174
184   *Zum gali, gali,* folk song   286

ADVANCED

113   *Beau soir,* Claude Debussy (to be prepared)   184
88   *Bewahret euch,* Wolfgang Amadeus Mozart   132
190   *Brave companion, a,* folk song   291
115   *Cage, the,* Charles Ives, (to be prepared)   192
126   *Cantata* I, Anton Webern (to be prepared)   222
177   *Dance of Zalongo,* folk song   279
117   *Der Tod,* Anton Webern   194
78   *Doux liens,* Francois Couperin (to be prepared)   120
134   *Each afternoon in Granada a child dies,* George Crumb   239
54   *Ecco morirò dunque,* Carlo Gesualdo (to be prepared)   70
39   *Entre vous, gentils amoureux,* Guillaume Dufay   48
75   *Et incarnatus est,* Johann Sebastian Bach   106
187   *Fare ye well, my darlin,* folk song   289
121   *God, the Lord shall be my light,* Arthur Honegger (to be prepared)   202
186   *John Henry,* folk song   288
38   *Kyrie eleison,* Guillaume Dufay (to be prepared)   46
92   *Lacrimoso son io,* Franz Schubert (to be prepared)   137
116   *Like a sick eagle,* Charles Ives (to be prepared)   193
125   *Mädel, was fangst Du jetzt an?* Alban Berg   218
79   *Ma voix,* Jean Philippe Rameau (to be prepared)   122
114   *Non ditemi nulla,* Giacomo Puccini (to be prepared)   187
52   *O magnum mysterium,* Thomás de Victoria   67
55   *O rôze reyne des fleurs,* Claude Lejeune   72
87   *Osanna in excelsis,* Wolfgang Amadeus Mozart (to be prepared)   130
103   *O tu che sei d'Osiride,* Giuseppe Verdi   161
189   *Rugged mountain slopes,* folk song   290
132   *Signpost* I, Eskil Hemberg   233
133   *Signpost* II, Eskil Hemberg   235
119   *Tears of autumn,* Bela Bartok (to be prepared)   197
122   *Thus spake Isaiah,* William Walton (to be prepared)   205
63   *Tremulo spirito,* Pietro Francesco Cavalli (to be prepared)   90
130   *Tre poemi (I),* Luigi Dallapiccola (to be prepared)   231
124   *Un Cygne,* Paul Hindemith   213

Foreword

Clearly, today's musical society is internationally mobile. Musicians are called upon to participate in varied, frequent concerts, often on different continents. Outstanding musical skills are required of the musician if he is to survive in today's musical market. Professional vocal and instrumental ensembles expect a high technical facility in sight reading. All major orchestral auditions require sight reading as a part of the audition process. More and more professional choruses do the same.

A musician must be a "fast-learn." There is greater demand for repertoire from all eras and the performer is expected to perform varied, difficult roles and parts, often with short rehearsal. Given the complexity and the difficulty of most new music, the musician without reading skills is at a great disadvantage. The non-reader, the slower learner, no matter how great his musical gift, is severely limited.

Musicians should work with the elements of music as if they were the mother tongue rather than a foreign language learned by rote as nonsense syllables. Pitches, rhythms, dynamics, and timbres must all be a natural part of our musical language. The inner ear of the musician should be developed to hear clearly without the actual sound of music. The development of the inner ear will ensure musical security and confidence, permitting freedom of expression and creativity. The deficient performer is always betrayed no matter how much rote learning has taken place.

The development of aural recognition by the inner ear is not the same as intellectual understanding. The non-musician can easily learn that a vertical sonority of C-E-G is a major triad, even that A-C-E$^\flat$-G$^\flat$ is a diminished seventh chord. The same is true of the intellectual understanding of musical form. The musician, however, must immediately translate and recognize all of these sonorities and forms into specific sounds and shapes.

Dimensions of Sight Singing is designed to fulfill precisely this function: to bridge the gap between theory and practice, to develop the indispensable inner ear, and to help transform the student of music into a musician. In the use of this book there are some simple procedures to follow which will facilitate learning:

Read Ahead
The student should read ahead, first a note or two, then larger and larger units. One should recognize large melodic, rhythmic units and execute them without looking a second time.

Breathe Fully
Take a full breath. Sound is vibrating air, and an ample supply is necessary in all ways. Involved discussion of breath support, although useful, is not obligatory for sight-reading lessons.

Sing Softly
Singing softly, for the initial reading, will allow the student to hear better and will make the process easier. Use a syllable for each note: loo loo loo . . .   or la la la . . . , etc.

Keep a Steady Tempo
A steady tempo is the foundation upon which reading music is based. If one does not know *when* to sing (rhythm), the *what* (pitch) cannot be securely produced.

Tap the Meter
While reading pitches and rhythms, lightly tap the meter. This coordination is requisite for good reading.

The technical skills of reading must, of course, be integrated with musical expression and structural understanding. Natural dynamics (crescendo and decrescendo) are integral to the shape of the melody, while articulation (staccato, legato, marcato, etc.) provides character for the musical line; both are absolutely essential to musical expressiveness. The structure of melody is illuminated by subtle variation of repeated units and by observing climax and denouement and appropriate conclusion (cadence).

Lastly, belief in the ability of the student to learn—and the student's belief in his own ability to succeed—are crucial to success.

Dr. Elmer Thomas
Director of Choral Organizations
College-Conservatory of Music
University of Cincinnati

Acknowledgments

So many persons have given generously of their time, advice, and encouragement to make this volume a reality. Among those a profound thanks is extended to Dean Jack Watson, who in the early 1970s gave support to the initial concept; to Dr. John Baur, for his superb first reading of the manuscript; to Ralph Holibaugh, to Elizabeth Bennett, and Richard Lavenda for their library sleuthing and general suggestions; to Anne Walters for many of the Latin translations and for her secretarial assistance; and to·C. E. Cooper for her Latin, Italian, French, and German translations, for her adroit editing, and for her unfailing support.

I am also most appreciative to the many publishers who have granted copyright permissions that these great moments in music history might be widely shared. Gordon Tren Anderson, my editor at Longman, and Gerald Warfield, music consultant, have advised wisely with consistent encouragement. To them both, I express my gratitude.

P.C.

Introduction

Song is one of man's most compelling and poignant communications. It predates recorded history by thousands of years; it frequently defines the aspirations and despairs of a people and their era; it forms the basis of ritual in every culture. It remains today a prime expressive force in pointing to societal moods and mores.

A generation ago, singing constituted a well-practiced participatory tradition in the church or synagogue, in public schools, in the home and in numerous social environments. Active participation has been a cornerstone of the proverbs of Western civilization, from Plato's philosophical admonitions to the contemporary tenets of cultural/social dynamics held since at least the Age of Enlightenment. This tradition apparently has been weakened in recent years. Personal involvement with music seems for the most part to be limited to the passive role of "aural spectator," whether in the concert hall or at the rock festival, in the discotheque or at the family reunion. The attendant psychological ramifications are perhaps speculative, yet persuasively demonstrable in several ways; and the most alarming of them, for the professional musician, is the increasing generation gap—if one may call it that—between the composer and the listener of the day.

Today, despite the complexity of much of contemporary music—making it too difficult for the amateur to perform in the home for pleasure—and the rhythmic and percussive rather than melodic orientation of some of rock and popular music, there nonetheless remains a vast literature from the past as well as numerous examples from today's music that are "singable." Singing is one of the few areas of active musical participation that continues to be both accessible and realistically attainable with a promise of positive personal rewards.

For the serious student of music, sight singing should be the *sine qua non* of musicianship. The physiological bases of music such as the length of a breath, the consistency of the heartbeat, and eye/ear sound correlations are dramatically underscored when one is singing. What one seeks in the acquisition of musicianship is the understanding and positive reinforcement of two interrelated psychological response mechanisms: inherent or instinctive responses, and learned responses induced by conditioning. Ultimately, of course, learned responses become "instinctive" as experience and insight are acquired. It is precisely here, in stimulating this conversion, that singing can assist in the nurturing of a substantial musicianship by providing:

1. An absolutely stable temporal-metric-rhythmic sense, both individually and in ensemble

2. An awareness and (eventually) keen accuracy of pitch *before* singing, playing, fingering—i.e., before the actual sounding of a specific note

3. An understanding of phrasing and phrase-structuring acquired by responding in physical and emotional terms to the requirements of vocal music

Organization and Purpose

Dimensions of Sight Singing consists of two parts spanning seventeen centuries of musical practice and offering representative samples of both art music and folk music for the unaccompanied and accompanied voice. The organization of this vast array of materials purports to serve pedagogical purposes as well as reflect historical continuity.

Part One consists of examples of Western vocal literature from the fourth century to the present. The arrangement is essentially chronological, for the purpose of illustrating stylistic changes as they occurred historically. Within this framework, a serious attempt has been made to order the material pedagogically from easy to difficult. Western music did not develop, however—and fortunately so—merely from a simple premise to one of ever-increasing complexity. The music of several eras responded to the complexity and mannerisms of a previous age by the imposition of restraints. For example: Music from the age of Haydn has fewer rhythmic and pitch problems than the music of the late Baroque period which preceded it. When studying music presenting fewer purely technical problems, the student is advised to strive for a perfect first reading in terms of intonation, rhythmic accuracy, phrasing, and rendering of text (when employed). However, in the presentation of music from the Classical era, an emphasis has been placed on the reading and use of C clefs, thus perhaps compensating for the less stringent technical demands of the examples. Moreover, in order to illustrate some of the diversity of material which every era produces, some difficult examples appear fairly early in the text. These are labeled "to be prepared." It goes without saying that not all music is instantly sight-readable at tempo by beginning students. These examples should be carefully prepared outside the classroom.

Original language texts have been included along with English translations or synopses. Language pronunciation guides for Latin, French, German, and Italian are provided in the appendix. Voice students and conducting majors as well as students of music history and music theory will certainly wish to consider utilization of original texts. However, the use of original language texts should be determined by the teacher and student and should be regarded as one of several approaches. Most schools of music will have a well-established and clearly defined methodology for sight singing:

1. fixed-do system
2. movable-do system
3. number system with the tonic note represented by "1"
4. use of vocalization syllables such as "loo" or "la"
5. other

Single-line melodies, canons, multi-voiced compositions, and accompanied songs are all included in *Dimensions of Sight Singing*. Utilization of the examples will be at the discretion of the teacher, determined by class goals and levels of class proficiency. Accompaniments which are included here have been carefully considered for technical feasibility for both teachers and students whose principal instrument is not the keyboard. It is suggested that these examples be sung with accompaniment only *after* having been learned without it, since the keyboard player would obviously provide both rhythmic and tonal "crutches" which can become an impediment to learning if indulged.

Part Two consists of examples of folk songs from both Western and non-Western cultures. Inasmuch as this body of literature ranges from simple to moderate in terms of difficulty, the ordering has been determined by the pitch resources of the melody—major scale, one of the minor scales, modal characteristics, pentatonic, etc. Because of the relatively uncomplicated technical demands of these melodies, the teacher and student may wish to *begin* initial studies with this portion of the book. Again, as in Part One, any of the solfeggio "systems" may be used. Many melodies include a suggested chordal background as accompaniment. Occasionally, these should be rendered by student participation at a keyboard instrument or guitar (lute, mandolin) or percussion instrument (vibraphone, marimba, bells). Part One should establish a basic musicianship and lead to a better understanding of the development of Western music and its stylistic changes. Part Two, although pedagogically serious, should also inject some welcome levity into a music theory class.

A Note of Explanation to Students and Teachers

Without question, *Dimensions of Sight Singing* poses many challenges. Comparable difficulties are met consistently by college music majors in orchestral and wind ensembles and in solo literature. A correspondingly rigorous training is not typically encountered by singers or in sight-singing classes in general.

Not every class will have equal numbers of sopranos, altos, tenors, and basses. A small class of women will obviously read only one or two lines of a complete SATB composition. In the very difficult examples, a number of sight-reading possibilities are imagined: (1) tap only the rhythm, (2) tap the rhythm and sing the first beat of each measure, (3) sing one line at a time doubled by an instrument (e.g. a clarinet), (4) assign the parts in advance to voice majors and have them "lead" the remainder of the class.

Again, the primary goals of this collection are to familiarize the student with the great folk and art music literature and to provide a framework for improving musicianship, particularly in the areas of rhythmic accuracy and pitch discernment. Concert-level performances are not envisioned. However, many of the examples are sufficiently within the grasp of music majors that the beauty of the music itself will be clearly transmitted.

As a pedagogical aid to both students and teachers, all examples are marked and indexed in three catagories: *Basic*, *Moderate*, and *Advanced*. The examples will help provide a foundation for both basic and advanced sight-singing programs.

PART ONE
How To Learn To Sight-Sing

Learning to sight-read requires patience and tenacity. It is a skill that is acquired rather slowly over an extended period of time. Sight reading must be practiced daily; there can be no real "cramming" the night before examinations. Tools of the trade include a metronome and a pitch pipe, both accurately calibrated.

As a general guide for learning the melodies presented in this book, Example 134 from Part Two is reproduced below with suggestions for how to approach the task step by step.

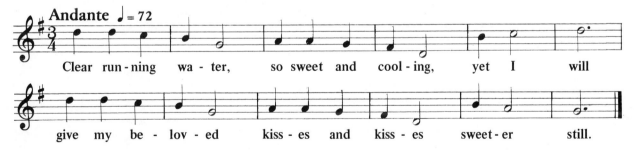

Zpěvy Domova. Jan Seidl. (L. Mazáč, Prague, 1943.) As published in *Folk Songs of Europe* edited by Maude Karpeles. Copyright 1956 by Novello & Company.

1. Scan the entire example, paying particular attention to the smallest note values. If, for example, measure 4 had contained sixteenth notes, then a slower basic pulse (tempo) might be required in order to sing the melody at a comfortable rate of speed throughout.

2. Consider: *clef*
   meter
   key signature
   basic mode (i.e., large third or small third; raised seventh; etc.)
   range

1

3. Establish the first pitch either by a pitch pipe or by a well-tuned piano (male voices, an octave lower).
4. Decide on the solfeggio system to be used—loo/la, fixed or movable do (see suggestion 1 on page 3)—or the text to which the melody was set.
5. Establish the basic pulse by tapping (left hand) or conducting patterns (right hand). Beat two full measures before beginning to sing.

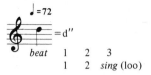

6. IMPERATIVES. For *first reading:* It is essential that the tempo be kept absolutely steady. If some pitches or rhythms are inaccurate on the first reading, DO NOT STOP. Continue to sing as many of the notes as possible—even if only the first note of each measure.
   Second reading: If the example is rhythmically complex, tap the rhythm separately without singing. Otherwise, correct pitch inaccuracies. Practice difficult interval leaps separately.
   Third reading: Add text (if requested by the teacher), and consider phrasing and dynamics.
7. The ultimate goal is, of course, to combine all steps so that the first reading achieves rhythmic and pitch accuracy, nuance of phrasing and dynamics, articulated consonants and vowels, and total musicality—a musicality that can be appreciated and enjoyed by the participant.

Solfeggio systems have been utilized for nearly a thousand years as an aid to interval memorization. Example 5, *Ut queant laxis,* quoted by Guido d'Arezzo (c. 1000) established the foundation for these procedures.

There are numerous "aural approaches," "ear training programs," "lab-tape complements," all of which strive to develop in the student the ability to hear, read, and accurately interpret the symbols of notation. A persistent and consistent sight-singing program will, in the author's opinion, be one of the most beneficial, with continued and lasting results, and musically enjoyable components of the music student's training.

It is to be emphasized again that sight singing is not the exclusive domain of the voice student, but rather an essential requisite of musicianship for all serious practitioners of the art.

Chapter 1
Early Sacred Chant

OBSERVATIONS

Examples 1–11 are drawn from diverse sources of early Christian monody from the fourth century to the thirteenth century, and deliberately include varied transcriptions. *Plainsong, plain chant,* and *cantus planus* are synonymous terms denoting a vast and beautiful literature worthy of serious study. From the second to the ninth centuries several types of chant flourished, including Christian plainsong taken directly from Hebrew chants, as well as Syrian, Byzantine, Ambrosian, Gregorian, Gallican, and Mozarabic chants. Eventually, however, following liturgical organization in the sixth century, Gregorian chant became the principal category and remained the primary musical force of Catholic ritual until the Second Vatican Council of 1962–65.

Chant is non-metric and uses a free prose rhythm following the Latin text. Plainsong is unaccompanied, has a limited range, and is typically modal. Notation for Gregorian chant was originally *neumatic* (that is, employing *neumes*, signs above the text indicating direction ∕, ∖, or ⌢, without benefit of a staff). The invention of the four-line staff is credited to Guido d'Arezzo around the year 1000. During the early thirteenth century, Gregorian (Roman) square-note notation became a standard format (see Example 2–A). Modern transcriptions vary somewhat, but the current practice favors the use

of a five-line staff with a treble clef *8va bassa* (to be sung an octave lower) 𝄞 , without meter but with short or full bar lines to denote punctuation of musical phrases.

Four types of text setting are observed, used singly or in combination:

1. *syllabic:* one note of melody for each syllable of text (Examples 1, 2, 3)
2. *neumatic:* a few notes for each syllable (Examples 5, 6, 7, 8, 9)
3. *psalmodic:* numerous syllables for each note or pitch (Example 11)
4. *melismatic:* numerous notes for each syllable (Example 10)

SUGGESTIONS

1. Example 1: Establish starting pitch and tempo (moderate). Read on a neutral syllable (*loo* or *la*). Read again with a solfeggio system (see below) and then with the Latin text, if so desired. The first and last notes (in this example, D) are the modal *finalis* **or** **modern** *tonic*; hence the example will accommodate diverse solfeggio systems. The first ten notes are shown:

Numbers:	1	1	5	7	7	2	1	7	1	1
Fixed do:	re	re	la	do	do	mi	re	do	re	re
Movable do (on *do*):	do	do	sol	te	te	re	do	te	do	do
Movable do (on *la*):	la	la	mi	sol	sol	ti	la	sol	la	la

2. Study the following chart for chant technique—with the thoroughness of the study to be determined by the teacher. Following the steps for learning Example 1 read Example 2b (modern notation), then compare it to Example 2a (Roman notation).

Clefs indicate the location of a particular pitch. Most common are the treble, or G clefs, and the bass, or F clefs. C clefs, used commonly in earlier music, are retained today for the viola and, on occasion, for the cello, bassoon, and trombone. Although all clefs are movable, one observes primarily the movable C clef.

Compare c and h.

Reprinted by permission of Harper & Row, Publishers, Inc.

*The notes and groups of notes (neumes) used in Gregorian chant appear on a four-line staff. Two clef signs are in use to indicate the relative pitch of the notes:

The *Do*-clef ![clef] shows on what line the note *Do* (C) is placed.

The *Fa*-clef ![clef] shows on what line the note *Fa* (F) is placed.

These clefs may appear on any line depending on the range of the melody to be sung, so that the notes of the piece may be placed on the staff lines and spaces, thus avoiding, as far as possible, the use of leger lines above or below the staff.

The *guide* ![guide] is a sign placed at the end of each line of Gregorian music to indicate in advance the first note of the following line. It is also employed in the course of a line when the extension of the melody demands a change in the place of the clef, to show the relative pitch of the first note after the change.

Three kinds of *bar-lines* are used:

The *double bar* ![bar] which indicates the end of a piece or a change of choir. The *full bar* ![bar] which indicates the end of a phrase and a full pause in the singing. The *half bar* ![bar] indicates divisions known as clauses or members, hence the half bar is also called the member bar. It cuts the two middle lines of the staff. The *quarter bar* ![bar] indicates divisions known as sections or incises. It cuts only the top line of the staff. The part played by each of these signs has to do with the punctuation of the musical phrase in respect to the greater rhythm of the piece. If a breath must be taken at either the half bar or the quarter bar, it must be taken off the value of the note before. The same holds true of the *comma* or *virgula*. ![comma] The only place for a stop or full pause in the singing is at the full bar or the double bar.

The only accidental permitted in the chant is the *flat* ♭, which may only be used on the note *si* (*ti*). The flat is effective only (1) as long as the word lasts, (2) until the next bar line of any kind, or (3) until revoked by the natural sign.

3. Sing the scalar form of all modes (Example 4), paying particular attention to half step/whole step relationships. It is observed that the authentic forms I, III, V, VII are very close to major or minor.

*Much of the following material from *Chants of the Church* published by the Gregorian Institute of America.

Dorian = natural minor with raised 6th
Phrygian = natural minor with lowered 2nd
Lydian = major with raised 4th
Mixolydian = major with lowered 7th

4. Examples 4–11 may present problems of intonation regarding whole steps and half steps. If poor intonation persists, work carefully at a well-tuned piano for short periods of time to correct the pitch problems.
5. Prepare Example 11 outside the classroom. Modern transcription is at the discretion of teacher and student.

1 BASIC   AMBROSIAN HYMN: Aeterne rerum conditor
c. 400 A.D.

Ae-ter-ne re-rum con-ditor, Noctem di-em-que qui re-gis,

Et tempo-rum das tem-po-ra, Ut al-le-ves fa-sti-di-um.

Eternal maker of all things

Eternal maker of all things, You who rule the night and day and give the seasons of the years to alleviate weariness.

Reproduced by permission of the publishers from *Historical Anthology of Music*, Vol. I, edited by Archibald T. Davison and Willi Apel, Cambridge, Mass.: Harvard University Press, copyright © 1974, 1977 by Alice D. Humez and Willi Apel.

2-A MODERATE   GREGORIAN CHANT (Roman notation): Victimae paschali laudes
11th century

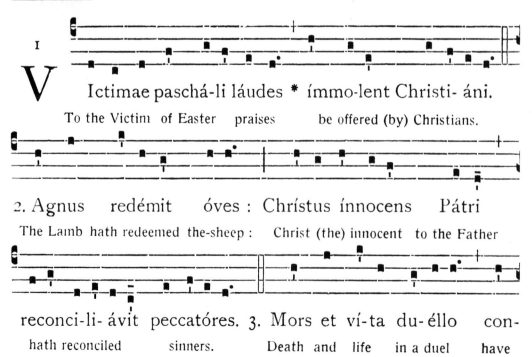

Ictimae paschá-li láudes * ímmo-lent Christi- áni.

To the Victim of Easter praises be offered (by) Christians.

2. Agnus redémit óves : Chrístus ínnocens Pátri

The Lamb hath redeemed the-sheep : Christ (the) innocent to the Father

reconci-li- ávit peccatóres. 3. Mors et ví-ta du-éllo con-

hath reconciled sinners. Death and life in a duel have

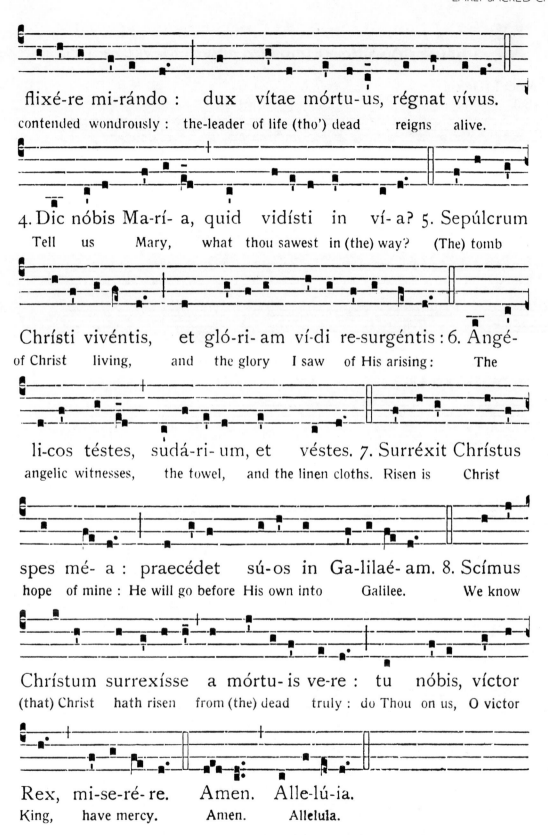

flixé-re mi-rándo :   dux   vítae mórtu-us, régnat vívus.
contended wondrously :   the-leader of life (tho') dead   reigns   alive.

4. Dic nóbis Ma-rí- a, quid vidísti in ví- a? 5. Sepúlcrum
Tell   us   Mary,   what thou sawest in (the) way? (The) tomb

Chrísti vivéntis,   et gló-ri- am ví-di re-surgéntis : 6. Angé-
of Christ   living,   and   the glory I saw of His arising: The

li-cos téstes, sudá-ri- um, et   véstes. 7. Surréxit Chrístus
angelic witnesses,   the towel, and the linen cloths. Risen is   Christ

spes mé- a : praecédet sú-os in Ga-lilaé- am. 8. Scímus
hope of mine : He will go before His own into   Galilee.   We know

Chrístum surrexísse a mórtu- is ve-re : tu   nóbis, víctor
(that) Christ   hath risen   from (the) dead   truly : do Thou on us, O victor

Rex, mi-se-ré- re.   Amen. Alle-lú-ia.
King,   have mercy.   Amen.   Allelula.

To the victim of Easter praises

2-B GREGORIAN CHANT (modern notation): Victimae paschali laudes

To the victim of Easter praises

3-A   GALLICAN CHANT: *Kyrie eleison*
BASIC

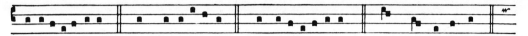

Ky-ri-e e-le-i-son.   Chri-ste e-le-i-son.   Ky-ri-e e-le-i-son.   Chri-ste au-di nos.

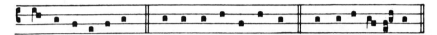

Chri-ste ex-au-di nos.   Pa-ter de cœ-lis De-us.   Mi-se-re-re no-bis.

3-B   GALLICAN CHANT: *Kyrie eleison*

Ky - ri - e   e - le - i - son.   Chri-ste   e - le - i - son.

Ky-ri - e   e-le-i-son.   Chri - ste   au-di nos.   Chri-ste ex-au-di nos.

Pa-ter de cœ - lis De - us.   Mi - se - re - re   no - - bis.

Lord have mercy

Lord have mercy. Christ have mercy.
Lord have mercy. Christ hear us.
Christ hear us. Father God of Heaven.
Have mercy on us.

4 The Medieval Church Modes

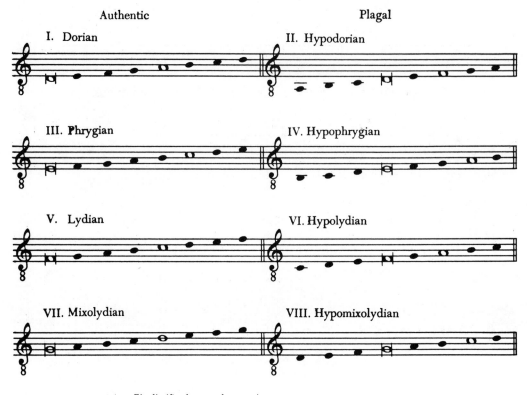

Authentic   Plagal

I. Dorian   II. Hypodorian

III. Phrygian   IV. Hypophrygian

V. Lydian   VI. Hypolydian

VII. Mixolydian   VIII. Hypomixolydian

ꞯ = *Finalis* (final note of repose)

o = *Psalm tone*, or *reciting tone*, or *confinalis*, also referred to as *dominant*.

5 GREGORIAN CHANT: Ut queant laxis

BASIC quoted by Guido d'Arezzo c. 990–1050

Ut que-ant la - xis *re*-so-na-re fi-bris *Mi* - ra ge-sto-rum *fa*-mu-li tu-o - rum,

Sol - ve pol-lu - ti *La* - bi-i re - a-tum, San - cte Jo-an-nes.

That they may freely

That Thy servants may freely sing forth the wonders of Thy deeds, remove all stain of guilt from their unclean lips, O Saint John.

6-A GREGORIAN CHANT: Deus, miserere
BASIC

Preces

De-us, mi-se-re-re, De-us mi-se-re-re, o Je-su bo-ne, tu il-li par-ce.   De-us mi-se-

-re - re.

© Oxford University Press 1954. Reprinted by permission.

6-B GREGORIAN CHANT: Deus, miserere

(Octave higher)

De - us, mi - se - re - re,   De - us mi - se - re - re,   o Je - su bo -

-ne,   tu il - li par - ce.   De - us   mi - se - re -   - re.

Lord, have mercy

Lord, have mercy. Lord, have mercy. O good Jesu, do thou spare him, Lord, have mercy.

© Oxford University Press 1954. Reprinted by permission.

7-A GREGORIAN CHANT: Insignis praeconiis
MODERATE

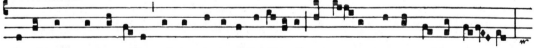

In-si-gnis præ-co-ni-is   al-mæ tu-æ no-bi-li-ta-ti con-so-nent vo-ces col-lau-dan-tes,

ver-bo sup-pli-ci pro-se-qua-mur: A - ve, in-cly-te mar-tyr.

© Oxford University Press 1954. Reprinted by permission.

7-B

In-si-gnis præ-co-ni-is al-mæ tu-æ no-bi-li-ta-ti

con-so-nent vo-ces col-lau-dan-tes, ver-bo sup-

-pli-ci pro-se-qua-mur: A-ve, in-cly-te mar-tyr.

With noble proclamation

Let the voices of them that praise thee ring out with noble proclamation in honour of thy bountiful dignity: let us follow on with the voice of prayer: Hail, illustrious martyr.

8-A GREGORIAN CHANT: *Aeterna christi munera*

BASIC

Ae-ter-na Chri-sti mu-ne-ra, A-po-sto-lo-rum glo-ri-am, Lau-des fe-ren-tes de-bi-

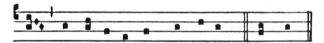

-tas, Læ-tis ca-na-mus men-ti-bus. A-men.

8-B GREGORIAN CHANT: *Aeterna christi munera*

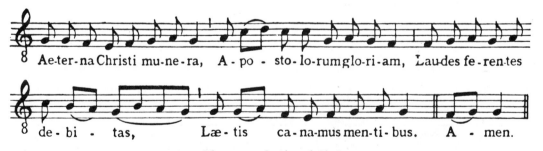

Ae-ter-na Christi mu-ne-ra, A-po-sto-lo-rumglo-ri-am, Lau-des fe-ren-tes

de-bi-tas, Læ-tis ca-na-mus men-ti-bus. A-men.

The eternal gifts of Christ

The eternal gifts of Christ the King,	And while due hymns of praise we pay,
The Apostles' glorious deeds we sing:	Our thankful hearts cast grief away.

9-A
BASIC

GREGORIAN CHANT: Heu, pius pastor

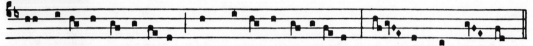

Heu, pi-us pas-tor oc-ci-dit, quem cul-pa nul-la in-fe-cit.   O   res plan-gen-da.

9-B
GREGORIAN CHANT: Heu, pius pastor

Heu,   pi - us   pa - stor   oc - ci   dit, quem cul - pa   nul -

-la   in - fe - cit.   O   res plan-gen - da

Alas, the Good Shepherd

Alas, the Good Shepherd is slain, whom no guilt stained. O mournful event!

10-A
BASIC

GREGORIAN CHANT: Mulier, quid ploras?

from The Easter Sepulchre Drama

Mu - li - er, quid plo- - -ras?

10-B
GREGORIAN CHANT: Mulier, quid ploras?

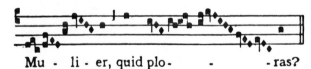

Mu - -li - er, quid plo- - - - -ras?

Woman, why weepest thou?

11 (to be prepared)
GREGORIAN CHANT: Kyrie eleison

MODERATE

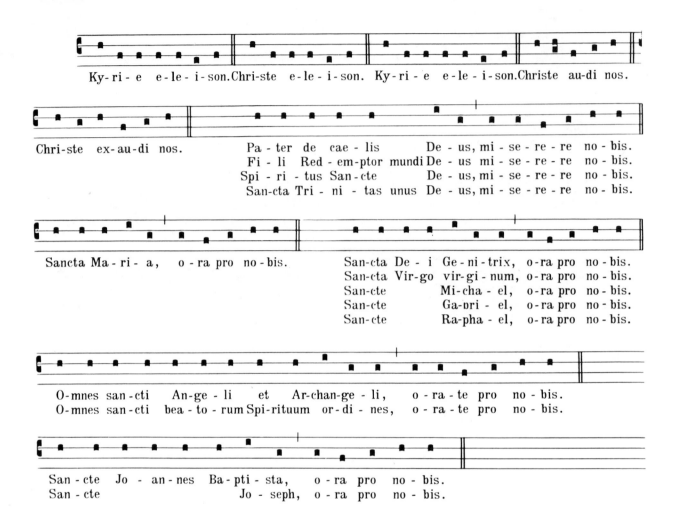

Ky-ri- e e-le- i-son. Chri-ste e-le-i-son. Ky-ri- e e-le-i-son. Christe au-di nos.

Chri-ste ex-au-di nos.

Pa - ter de cae - lis De - us, mi - se - re - re no - bis.
Fi - li Red - em-ptor mundi De - us mi - se - re - re no - bis.
Spi - ri - tus San - cte De - us, mi - se - re - re no - bis.
San-cta Tri - ni - tas unus De - us, mi - se - re - re no - bis.

Sancta Ma - ri - a, o - ra pro no - bis.

San-cta De - i Ge - ni - trix, o - ra pro no - bis.
San-cta Vir-go vir-gi - num, o - ra pro no - bis.
San-cte Mi-cha - el, o - ra pro no - bis.
San-cte Ga-bri - el, o - ra pro no - bis.
San-cte Ra-pha - el, o - ra pro no - bis.

O-mnes san -cti An-ge - li et Ar-chan-ge - li, o - ra-te pro no - bis.
O-mnes san -cti bea - to - rum Spi-rituum or-di - nes, o - ra-te pro no - bis.

San - cte Jo - an - nes Ba - pti - sta, o - ra pro no - bis.
San - cte Jo - seph, o - ra pro no - bis.

Lord have mercy

Lord have mercy on us. Christ have mercy on us. Lord have mercy on us. Christ hear us. Christ *hear* us. God the Father of Heaven, have mercy on us.

God the Son, Redeemer of the world, etc.
God the Holy Spirit, etc.
Holy Trinity one God, etc.

Holy Mary, pray for us. Holy Mother of God pray for us
Holy Virgin of Virgins, etc.
Holy Michael, etc. Holy Gabriel, etc.
Holy Raphael, etc.

All ye holy angels and archangels, pray for us.
All ye holy ranks of blessed Spirits, etc.
Holy John the Baptist, etc. Holy Joseph, etc.

FURTHER SUGGESTED STUDIES

Devise interval studies such as the following to perfect intonation:

1. From Example 1

2. From Example 2

3. From Example 8

Make sure the pitch is "high" enough.

4. From Example 10

Practice this series at different pitch levels, e.g.:

Chapter 2
Organum; Polyphony through the Ars Antiqua

OBSERVATIONS

Many scholars have conjectured that the development of polyphony—more than one line of music performed simultaneously—was the most important innovation in the entire history of Western music. Numerous theories persist as to the origins of polyphony, but consensus seems to indicate that the practice of singing in parallel perfect fourths or perfect fifths (*organum*) contributed most significantly. Examples 12–16 illustrate two main categories of *organa* and provide excellent opportunities for the student of sight singing to work with one or two colleagues to achieve accurate intonation.

Examples 18–19 are two- and three-voice polyphonic compositions where contrary motion between the voices is the ideal and where most simple intervals are found. In Example 18 the two lines musically "reflect" each other in near mirror images. The *polyphonic conductus* (Example 19) was an important form of this era. It utilized a freely composed tenor rather than that of plainsong, and typically had a uniform rhythm with all voices (two or three) singing the same text. In the polylingual motet constructed on *Hec Dies* (Example 21), the complexities of rhythm, intervals, and text require a most careful attention to detail.

SUGGESTIONS

1. It is suggested that Examples 12–15 be used as intonation studies in which the most careful listening is practiced by the singers. Have two students (or four in Example 15) perform, using the syllable *la* or *loo*, while the remainder of the class notes pitch and intonation inaccuracies; this may be beneficial to both singing and ear training.
2. Examples 19 and 20 may pose the first metric and rhythmic difficulties presented in this text. Since the original of Example 19 was without bar lines of any kind, the present transcription opts for a $\frac{3}{2}$ meter with a bar line every four measures. A dotted line (actual or mental) may assist in performance, as shown here:

The syncopated triplet must be accurate. It is suggested that the student anticipate the triplet by subdividing the ♩ into triplets:

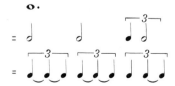

12 PARALLEL ORGANUM: Rex caeli, Domine

BASIC° 9th century

Rex coe-li Do- mi- ne ma-ris un-di-so-ni
Ti- ta-nis ni-ti-di squa-li-di-que so-li,

Te hu-mi-les fa- mu-li mo-du-lis ve-ne-ran-do pi-is
Se ju-be-as fla-gi-tant va-ri- is li- be-ra-re ma-lis.

King of Heaven

King of Heaven, Lord alone of the wave-sounding sea, of the shining sky and of
the rough earth.
Your humble servants do entreat you with dutiful adoration
To command that they be freed from sundry evils.

13 ORGANUM AT THE FIFTH: Sit Gloria Domini

BASIC 9th century
from *Musica Enchiriadis*

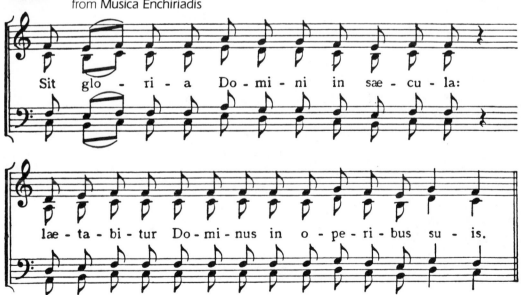

Sit glo - ri - a Do - mi - ni in sae - cu - la:

lae - ta - bi - tur Do - mi - nus in o - pe - ri - bus su - is.

May the glory of the Lord

May the glory of the Lord abide for ever: the Lord shall rejoice in his works.

14 BASIC MELISMATIC ORGANUM: Benedicamus Domino
11th century
School of St. Martial

Be _____

ne _____

di _____

ca _____

mus _____

(etc.)

Let us praise the Lord

Let us praise, etc.

15 BASIC ORGANUM IN THIRDS: Nobilis, humilis, Magne
12th century

No-bi-lis, hu-mi-lis, Magne, martyr sta-bi-lis,   Et tu-tor lau-da-bi-lis, tu-os sub-di-tos
Ha-bi-lis, u-ti-lis, co-mes ve-ne-   ra-bi-lis

Ser-va car-nis fra-gi-lis mo-le po-si-tos.

Noble, humble Magnus

Noble, humble Magnus, steadfast martyr, Skillful, helpful, worthy companion
and excellent defender, Protect thy servants who are weighed down by their
weak flesh.

16 MELISMATIC ORGANUM: Benedicamus Domino

MODERATE Leonin (active c. 1160–1180)
School of Notre Dame

Let us praise the Lord.

17 CONDUCTUS: Beata viscera

MODERATE Perotin (c. 1160–1220

Be- a- ta vi- sce- ra Ma-ri- e vir-gi- nis, Ve- ste sub al- te- ra vim ce- lans nu-mi-nis, Di- cta- vit fe- de-
cu- jus ad u- be- ra rex ma- gni no-mi- nis,
ra De- i et ho- mi- nis. O
mi- ra no- vi- tas et no-vum gau- di- um, Ma-
tris in-te- gri-tas post
pu- er- pe- ri- um.

Blessed womb

Blessed womb of the Virgin Mary, at whose bosom a King noble in name, concealing the might of his godhead beneath other raiment, has declared the covenant of God and man. O wonderful strangeness and new joy, the purity of the Mother after the birth of the Child.

18

MODERATE

HYMN: Excerpt from Mira Lege, Miro Modo
12th century

Suggested tempo: o· = c. 60–72

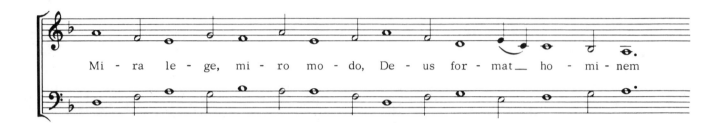

Mi - ra le - ge, mi - ro mo - do, De - us for - mat_ ho - mi - nem

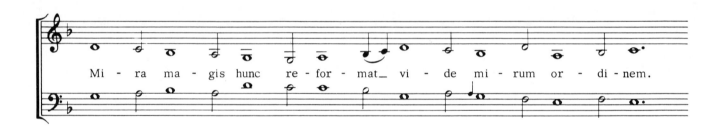

Mi - ra ma - gis hunc re - for - mat_ vi - de mi - rum or - di - nem.

By wondrous law, in wondrous fashion

By wondrous law, in wondrous fashion, God directs man.
By much more wondrous law He transforms him,
Behold this wondrous order.

19

MODERATE

HYMN: Nato Nobis Hodie
13th century
in *Conductus* style

Na - to no - bis ho - di - e   de Ma - ri - a vir - gi - ne

e - ter - no re - gi glo - ri - ae   cum su - a - vi

iu - bi - lo De - o di - ca - mus gra - ti - as.

Born to us this day

With grateful jubilation let us give thanks to God for the eternal king of glory
born to us this day of the Virgin Mary.

20 MODERATE

(to be prepared)
MOTET: O mitissima (Quant voi) — Virgo — Hec dies
13th century

♩. = c. 72

*Quant voi re-ve-nir D'es-té la sai - son,

O mi-tis-si-ma Vir-go Ma - ri - a,

Vir - go vir - gi - num, Lu-men lu - mi - num, **

Hec

Que le bois font re-ten-tir Tuit cil oi - sil -

Pos-ce tu-um fi - li - um Ut no - bis au -

Re-for-ma-trix ho - mi - num, Que por-ta-sti

di - - -

lon, A - donc pleur et sou - pir

xi - li - um Det___ et re-me - di - um

Do-mi - num, Per te, Ma - ri - a,

es Hec

*Note that the top voice may sing either the Latin or French text.　　**See page 16 for an explanation of 2 ♫ against 3 ♫♩

O most mild (When I see)

O mitissima: O Virgin Mary most mild,
Beseech thy Son
To grant unto us support and succor
Against the deceptive crafts of evil spirits
And against their wickednesses.

Virgo virginum: Virgin of virgins, Light of lights,
Reformer of men, Who hast borne the Lord,
Let pardon be bestowed through you, Mary,
As the angel announced: Thou art a virgin
before and after.

Hec dies (Haec dies): This is the day . . .

Quant voi: When I see the season of summer return,
that makes the woods resound with all the
little birds,
then I cry and sigh with the great desire
I have for the beautiful Marion,
Who holds my heart prisoner.

FURTHER SUGGESTED STUDIES

1. Practice interval intonation by playing one pitch on a well-tuned piano while singing a different pitch.

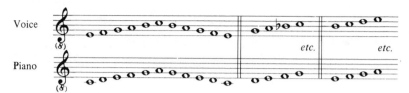

2. Measure 5 of Example 20 contains an example of 2 against 3. An important skill of musicianship for all serious performers, but especially for conductors and keyboard-ists, is the ability to tap or conduct one rhythm with one hand and a different one with the other hand. Again subdivision using a common denominator (in this case, 6) yields results:

When combining the two voices, using the count of 6, the top voice sounds at the count of 1 and 4, and the middle voice sounds at the count of 1, 3, and 5. This method provides an exact combination.

Chapter 3
Secular Songs from the Eleventh to Fourteenth Centuries

OBSERVATIONS

From about the end of the tenth century, secular monophony developed as a derived but separate branch of music from plainsong. These secular melodies were typically metrical, contained regular phrases, and were not strictly modal. Nearly 2,000 melodies are extant by troubadours, trouvères, Minnesinger, and goliards—the latter group consisting mainly of students who roamed Europe composing and singing songs about love, drinking, and bawdy adventures. (A comparison to twentieth-century rock groups is tempting.)

With the exception of the goliards' songs, which were typically in Latin, secular monophony was in the vernacular. The element of rhythm became equal in importance to that of pitch during this era.

SUGGESTIONS

1. Examples 22–28 present no special problems of pitch. Solfeggio systems may be profitably used. The French or German text may be substituted later. Rhythms must be precise and may require the method of subdivision discussed at the end of Chapter 2.
2. Example 26 contains a division of the beat into five equal parts, called a quintuplet:

A natural tendency is to rush and then wait for the second beat. To avoid this rhythmic inaccuracy, be sure to tap both beats:

Once the passage is rhythmically exact, remove the accents.
3. *Le Jeu de Robin et Marion* (Example 27) is included as a possible class project. Voice majors or small groups of students may wish to prepare the "play" for presentation in class. Voice parts may be doubled by instruments, such as flute, oboe, viola, and cello. Percussionists may wish to improvise additional parts; tenor drum and tambourines are appropriate for the style.

Examples 29-A and 29-B show two transcriptions of the same melody. Both are valid. 29-B is a more recent transcription and is appreciably more fluent rhythmically.

GOLIARD SONG: O Roma nobilis
11th century

O noble Rome

O noble Rome, orb and ruler,
most excellent of cities,
red with the rosy blood of martyrs
and pale with the white lilies of the Virgin;
We wish you health forever
We bless you: Hail through the centuries!

From *Examples of Music Before 1400* edited by Harold Gleason. Copyright © 1942 by F.S. Crofts & Co., Inc. Reprinted by permission of Harold Gleason.

RONDEAU: Vos n'aler
Guillaume d'Amiens (13th century)

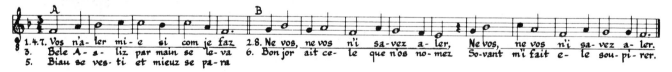

You don't live

(1) *You don't live as I do.*
　　(2) *Nor do you know how to live thus.*
　　Nor do you know how to live thus.
(3) Fair Alice arose one morning,
(4) *You don't live as I do.*
(5) Dressed herself fairly and decked herself better.
　　(6) Good-day to her whom I dare not name;
　　Often she makes me sigh.
(7) *You don't live as I do.*
　　(8) *Nor do you know how to live thus,*
　　Nor do you know how to live thus.

Reproduced by permission of the publishers from *Historical Anthology of Music*, Vol. I, edited by Archibald T. Davison and Willi Apel, Cambridge, Mass.: Harvard University Press, copyright © 1974, 1977 by Alice D. Humez and Willi Apel.

23
BASIC

VIRELAI: C'est la fin
Guillaume d'Amiens (13th century)

This is the end

(1) *This is the end, no matter what be said:*
   I shall love.
   (2) It is down there amidst the fields.
   (3) This is the end, I wish to love.
(4) Games and dances are being held there,
   A fair friend have I.
(5) *This is the end, no matter what be said:*
   I shall love.

Reproduced by permission of the publishers from *Historical Anthology of Music,* Vol. I, edited by Archibald T. Davison and Willi Apel, Cambridge, Mass.: Harvard University Press, copyright © 1974, 1977 by Alice D. Humez and Willi Apel.

24
BASIC

VIRELAI: Or la truix
Trouvère song (12th–13th century)

Reproduced from *Masterpieces of Music Before 1750,* compiled and edited by Carl Parrish and John F. Ohl, by permission of W.W. Norton & Company, Inc. Copyright 1951 by W.W. Norton & Company, Inc. Copyright renewed 1979 by John F. Ohl and Catherine C. Parrish.

tre   cer - tains   de ceu   ke n'a_____ve - rai_____ des
was   so   sure   of that   which I_____ shan't have_____ so

mois, oix, oix! C'est ceu   ke plus_____ me ble_____
soon, a - las! 'Tis most - ly that_____ which hurts_____

ce. Or la   truix trop_____ du - re_____te, voir,
me. I find   it hard_____ to woo_____her, in -

voir! A ceu k'elle est_____ sim - ple_____te.
deed! Be - cause she is_____ so sim_____ple.

25 BASIC RONDEAU: En ma dame
Perrin d'Agincourt (13th century)

In my lady

(1) *In my lady I have placed my heart*
    (2) *And my mind.*
(3) I shall not leave her for any reason:
(4) *In my lady I have placed my heart.*
(5) I was overcome by her grey eyes
    (6) Laughing and clear:
(7) *In my lady I have placed my heart*
    (8) *And my mind.*

When I see at the end

At the end of the summer when I see the leaves fall
And the great prettiness of the birds come to an end,
Then I feel a desire to sing greater than is my wont.
For she to whom I give myself loyally has ordered me to sing;
Therefore I shall: and when my lady pleases, I shall have joy.

27 DRAMATIC PASTORAL: Le Jeu de Robin et Marion

MODERATE

Adam de la Halle (c. 1230–c. 1288)

Text: Adam de la Halle

*The original "nonsense syllables" have been retained.

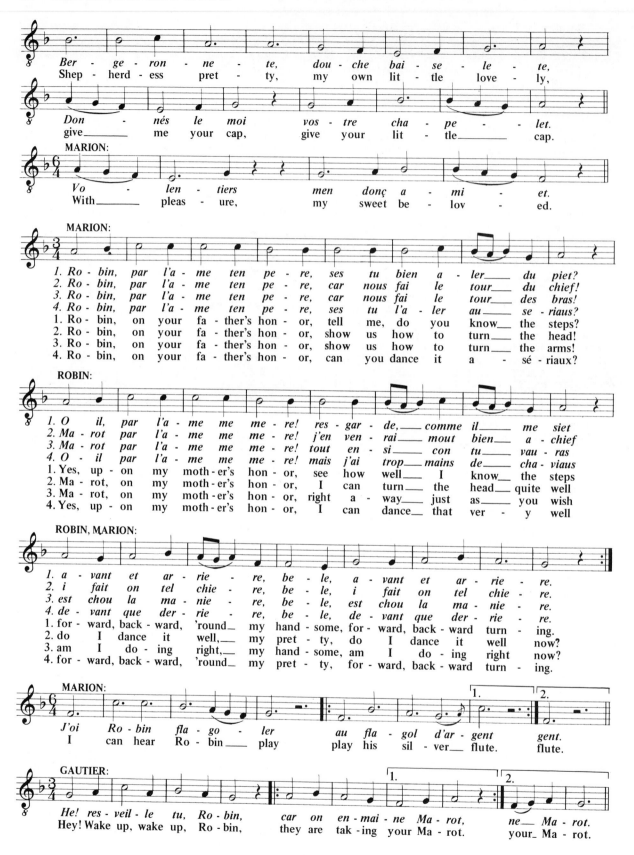

Ber - ge - ron - ne - te, dou - che bai - se - le - te,
Shep - herd - ess pret - ty, my own lit - tle love - ly,

Don - nés le moi vos - tre cha - pe - let.
give_____ me your cap, give your lit - tle cap.

MARION:

Vo - len - tiers men donç a - mi - et.
With_____ pleas - ure, my sweet be - lov - ed.

MARION:

1. Ro - bin, par l'a - me ten pe - re, ses tu bien a - ler_____ du piet?
2. Ro - bin, par l'a - me ten pe - re, car nous fai le tour_____ du chief!
3. Ro - bin, par l'a - me ten pe - re, car nous fai le tour_____ des bras!
4. Ro - bin, par l'a - me ten pe - re, ses tu l'a - ler au_____ se - riaus?
1. Ro - bin, on your fa - ther's hon - or, tell me, do you know_ the steps?
2. Ro - bin, on your fa - ther's hon - or, show us how to turn_ the head!
3. Ro - bin, on your fa - ther's hon - or, show us how to turn_ the arms!
4. Ro - bin, on your fa - ther's hon - or, can you dance it a - sé - riaux?

ROBIN:

1. O il, par l'a - me me me - re! res - gar - de,_____ comme il_____ me siet
2. Ma - rot par l'a - me me me - re! j'en ven - rai_____ mout bien_____ a - chief
3. Ma - rot par l'a - me me me - re! tout en - si_____ con tu_____ vau - ras
4. O il par l'a - me me me - re! mais j'ai trop_ mains de_____ cha - viaus
1. Yes, up - on my moth - er's hon - or, see how well_ I know_ the steps
2. Ma - rot, on my moth - er's hon - or, I can turn_ the head_ quite well
3. Ma - rot, on my moth - er's hon - or, right a - way_ just as_ you wish
4. Yes, up - on my moth - er's hon - or, I can dance_ that ver - y well

ROBIN, MARION:

1. a - vant et ar - rie - re, be - le, a - vant et ar - rie - re.
2. i fait on tel chie - re, be - le, i fait on tel chie - re.
3. est chou la ma - nie - re, be - le, est chou la ma - nie - re.
4. de - vant que der - rie - re, be - le, de - vant que der - rie - re.
1. for - ward, back - ward, 'round_ my hand - some, for - ward, back - ward turn - ing.
2. do I dance it well,_ my pret - ty, do I dance it well now?
3. am I do - ing right,_ my hand - some, am I do - ing right now?
4. for - ward, back - ward, 'round_ my pret - ty, for - ward, back - ward turn - ing.

MARION:

J'oi Ro - bin fla - go - ler au fla - gol d'ar - gent gent.
I can hear Ro - bin_ play play his sil - ver_ flute. flute.

GAUTIER:

He! res - veil - le tu, Ro - bin, car on en - mai - ne Ma - rot, ne_ Ma - rot.
Hey! Wake up, wake up, Ro - bin, they are tak - ing your Ma - rot. your_ Ma - rot.

ROBIN:

1. J'ai en - core un tel pas - té qui n'est: mi - e de las - té
2. Que jou ai un tel ca - pon qui a gros et gras cre - pon
1. I still have a mor - sel left it's not bad; just wait and see;
2. And a ca - pon I have too with a fat and juic - y comb;

1., 2. que nous man - ge - rons, Ma - ro - te, bec a bec et moi et vous
1., 2. we will eat it my Ma - ro - te, nose to nose just you and I

1., 2. chi me ra - ten - dés, Ma - ro - te, chi ven - rai par - ler a vous.
1., 2. pro - mise you will wait, Ma - ro - te, I'll come back to talk to you.

THE COMPANY:

A - veuc te - le com - pai - gni - e doit on bien joi - e me - ner.
One can on - ly live in___ plea - sure in such mer - ry___ com - pa - ny.

28

BASIC

MINNELIED: Willekommen mayenschein
Neidhardt von Reuenthal c. 1180–c. 1240

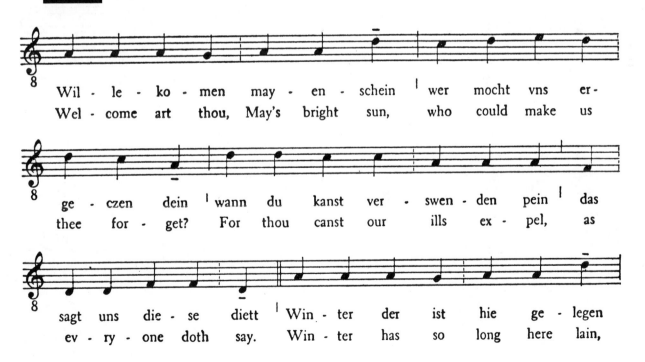

Wil - le - ko - men may - en - schein wer mocht vns er -
Wel - come art thou, May's bright sun, who could make us

ge - czen dein wann du kanst ver - swen - den pein das
thee for - get? For thou canst our ills ex - pel, as

sagt uns die - se diett Win - ter der ist hie ge - legen
ev - ry - one doth say. Win - ter has so long here lain,

auff dem velde vnd in den wegen | wil-lig-lich gab
on the fields and in the paths; that he fain would

er den segen | da er von hyn-nen schiett | Nun wil-tu die
bless us all and hence from here de-part. Now wilt thou the

hai-de a-ber e-ren | und wilt klei-ne vo-ge-lein dein
wood-land fill with blos-som; and wilt teach the lit-tle birds thy

sus-se sti-me le_____ren | das sie in dem
mel-o-dies so love_____ly, so that all the

wal-de | pal-de | irn sus-se sank ge-me-ren.
woods and mea-dows will ring with their sweet sing-ing.

Welcome, May's bright sun

29-A
BASIC

MINNELIED: Mayenzeit one neidt
Neidhart von Reuental

1. May-en-zeit o-ne neidt freu-den geit wi-der streit. 2.Sein wi-der-ku-men
3. Uff dem plan o-ne wan sicht man stan wol-ge-than 4. Lich-te präu-ne

kan uns al-len hel-ffen. 5. Durch das gras sind sie schon uf ge-drun-gen, 6. Und der walt
plüm-lein bey den ge-ffen.

ma-nig-valt   un-ge-tzalt   ist der schalt. 7. Das er ward mit dem nie bas ge _ sun-gen.

29-B
BASIC

MINNELIED: *Maienzit Ane nit*
Neidhart von Reuental

(A) 1
Mai - en - zit   A - ne nit   Vröu - den git   Wi - der strit: Sin

2
wi - der - ku - men kan   uns al - len hel-___ fen.   **(A)** 3 Uf dem plan

A - ne wan   Sicht man stan   Wol - ge - tan   4 Lieh - tiu bru - niu

bleum - lin bi den gel-___ fen.   **(B)** 5 Durch das gras sint si schon uf -

- ge - drun - gen.   **(A)** 6 Und der walt   Ma - nih - valt   Un - ge - zalt   Ist

7
er - schalt,   Daz er wart   mit dem   nie baz   ge - sun-___ gen.

Maytime, without envy

Maytime, without envy,
Happy time, adverse to strife,
Has returned with solace for us all.

On the meadow, without wile,
One can see, pleasingly,
light brown little flowers
next to the yellow ones.

Through the grass they have pushed up,
and the woods, manifold uncounted,
have resounded that there waits
with whom none has sung.

Transcribed by Edith Borroff. Used by permission.

30 BAR FORM: Nû al'erst
MODERATE

Walther von der Vogelweide c. 1170–c. 1230

1. Nu al-erst lebe ich mir wer-de Sit min sün-dic ou-ge siht.
2. Hie daz land und auch die er-de Den man vil der e-ren giht.
3. Mirst ge-schehen des ich je bat:

Ich bin kom-men an die stat Da got men-nisch-li-chen trat.

Now at last

(1) Now at last my life seems worth while
Now that my sinful eyes behold
(2) Here the land and soil
Which men hold in such high honor.
(3) I have attained that for which
I so often prayed:
I have set foot on the spot
That God in human form has trod.

31 SONG: Ich setze
MODERATE

Walther von der Vogelweide

Ich   set - ze

mi - nen   vuz   An   des   sum - mers

kle   Die   da

was   ghe - - - - stalt.

I set

I set my foot on the summer clover which was placed there.

32 ROUND: Sumer is icumen in
MODERATE (c. 1310)

FURTHER SUGGESTED STUDIES

1. Devise rhythmic studies with varying subdivisions of the beat.
   For example:

   Then add a second part:

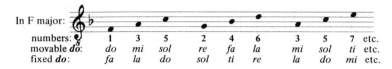

2. Sing major and minor scales, paying particular attention to the 6th and 7th scale degrees for perfect intonation.
3. Sing a succession of arpeggiated triads, using numbers and syllables.

In F major:									
numbers:	1	3	5	2	4	6	3	5	7 etc.
movable *do*:	do	mi	sol	re	fa	la	mi	sol	ti etc.
fixed *do*:	fa	la	do	sol	ti	re	la	do	mi etc.

Chapter 4

Sacred and Secular Music from the Fourteenth and Fifteenth Centuries

OBSERVATIONS

The fourteenth century is known for the *Ars Nova*, a period of pronounced activity in secular music. Guillaume de Machaut and Francesco Landini were the principal composers, while Petrarca, Dante, Boccaccio, and Chaucer added new dimensions to vernacular literature.

New polyphonic forms were invented and canon and imitation were used extensively. Perhaps the most important developments in music were those pertaining to rhythm. Duple time (*tempus imperfectum*) became acceptable (see Example 39); *hocket* (alternation of melody and rests between two voices) was used as a rhythmic embellishment and the constructive device known as *isorhythm* served as the unifying factor of many motets. Rhythmic freedom prevailed, and as a result the period yielded some of the most complex music ever composed. Only in the latter half of the twentieth century has rhythmic complexity been equal to that of the *Ars Nova*.

From about 1250, a new system of notation was developed, which is termed *mensural* notation. The new five-line system provided for precision of both pitch and duration. Until about 1450 *black mensural* was used, and thereafter, until about 1600, *white mensural* was the principal notational system. Organ and lute tablatures, however, were of a very different kind, responding to different requirements of the composer.

The Burgundian and Flemish schools dominated the fifteenth century and were rivaled only by important activities in England. Three-voice polyphony prevailed; the interval of the third assumed new importance both melodically and vertically. The parallelism of *organum* had long disappeared and was replaced by new kinds of parallelisms referred to as *fauxbourdon* and *English discant*. In both, the results yield chords of first inversion, i.e., with the third of the chord in the lowest voice.

SUGGESTIONS

1. The examples in this chapter will pose two main problems. Several melodies will, at some points, be "out of range." The suggested solution for this problem is to transpose the entire piece. For instance, Example 33 may be sung a perfect fifth lower for basses and altos, starting on notes c and c'.

   The other problems are related to meter and rhythm. Numerous syncopations occur, as well as the shifting of main accents within the bar (such as the shift from two to three in $\frac{6}{8}$ time), as in Example 39:

   In the varied transcriptions, the eighth note is constant.

2. It is suggested that Examples 37, 38, and 39 be first approached as rhythmic exercises with the class divided into groups, each precisely tapping and *counting* the notes of its assigned part.

3. "Fixed-do" solfeggio will be easier than "movable-do" for the Machaut and Landini examples. Dunstable and Dufay, with strong tonal orientations, will accommodate either system.

4. The two lower voices of Examples 37 and 40 may be assigned to two cellos or to viola and cello. Student conductors may be profitably, if not gainfully, employed!

   NOTE: Examples 36, 39, and 40 use "partial signatures," a common notational procedure of the time. The practice simply amounts to a different key signature in each melodic line. Except for an awareness of the signature for the specific line, the procedure should cause no problem in sight reading for the student.

33 BASIC **VIRELAI:** Comment qu'a moy
Guillaume de Machaut (c. 1304–1377)

1.5. Com-ment qu'a moy lon- tein- ne soi- es, da-me d'on-nour, si mi-estes vous pro- chein- ne par pen-ser nuit et jour.
4. vo ma-nie-re cer-tein-ne et vo fre-sche cou-lour qui n'est pa-le ne vein-ne, voy tou-dis sans se- jour.

2. Car Sou-ve-nir me mein-ne, si qu'a-des sans se- jour
3. vo biau-te sou-ve-rein-ne, vo gra-ci-eus a- tour,

Although from me

(1) *Although you are far from me, my noble lady,*
   Still you are near to me in thought, night and day.

(2) For memory so leads me that always without respite
(3) Your soverign beauty, your gracious appearance,
(4) Your sure manner and your fresh color—
   Neither pale nor ruddy—I see always without respite.

(5) *Although you are far from me, my noble lady,*
   Still you are near to me in thought, night and day. (3 stanzas)

34 BASIC (to be prepared)
VIRELAI: Plus dure
Machaut

1.5. Plus du- re que un dy-a- mant ne que pier-re d'a- y-mant est vo dur- té, da- me qui n'a-
4. par un ac- cueil at-trai- ant, m'ont au cuer en re- sgar-dant si fort na- vré que ja mais joi-

ves pi- té, de vostre a- mant qu'o- ci- es en de- si- rant vostre a- mi- tié.
e n'a- vré, ju- sques a- tant que vo gra- ce qu'il a- tant m'au- res don- né.

2.Da- me, vo pu- re biau-té qui tou-tes passe, a mon gré, et vo sam-blant
3.simple et plein d'u- mi- li- té, de dou-ceur fi- ne pa- ré, en sous-ri- ant,

Harder

(1) *Harder than a diamond*   Lady, who feel no pity
   Or a lodestone   For your lover whom you kill
   Is your harshness,   As he desires your friendship.

That never shall I have joy
Until you shall have given me
Your grace.

(5) *Harder than a diamond*
Or a lodestone
Is your harshness,
Lady, who feel no pity
For your lover whom you kill
As he desires your friendship.

(2) Lady, your pure beauty,
Which surpasses all—so I feel—
And your appearance,

(3) Simple and modest,
Bedecked with fine sweetness,
Smiling,

(4) And with an attractive welcome
Have wounded me so deeply in the heart
As I looked at you

35 BASIC — BALLATA: Angelica biltà
Francesco Landini (1325–1397)

Angelic beauty

1, 5. Angelic beauty has come to earth.
2. May each who loves to see beauty, virtue, charm, and grace
3. Come to behold her who alone is loveliness, though he will have of her—as does my soul—.
4. No peace, I think, for all the anguish.

36 MODERATE MASS: Gloria in excelsis
Worcester School (14th century)

Et in ter-ra pax ho-mi-ni-bus bo-ne vo-lun-ta-tis. Lau-da-mus te. Be-ne-di-ca-mus te. Ad-o-

ra-mus te. Glo-ri-fi-ca-mus te. Gra-ti-as a-gi-mus ti-bi propter magnam glo-ri-am tu-am, Do-mi-ne

De-us rex coe-le-stis De-us Pa-ter om-ni-po-tens. Do-mi-ne fi-li u-ni-ge-ni-

te Je-su Chri-ste. Do-mi-ne De-us, A-gnus De-i, fi-li-us Pa-tris.

Glory to the highest

And on earth peace to men of good will. We praise you, we bless you. We worship you. We glorify you. We give thanks to you for your great glory, Lord God, heavenly King, God the Father almighty. Lord the only-begotten Son Jesus Christ. Lord God, Lamb of God; Son of the Father.

37 (to be prepared)
HYMN: Beata Mater
MODERATE John Dunstable (c. 1385–1453)

From *Musica Britannica—A National Collection of Music, Volume VIII: John Dunstable Complete Works* edited by Manfred F. Bukofzer. Second revised edition prepared by Margaret Bent, Ian Bent and Brian Troell. Copyright 1953 by The Royal Musical Association & The American Musicological Society. Revised edition © 1970. Reprinted by permission of Galaxy Music Corporation.

Blessed Mother

Blessed Mother and unblemished Virgin,
Glorious Queen of the world. Intercede for us
with the Lord.

38 (to be prepared)
MASS: Kyrie eleison
ADVANCED Guillaume Dufay (c. 1400–1474)
from Missa: Sancti Jacobi

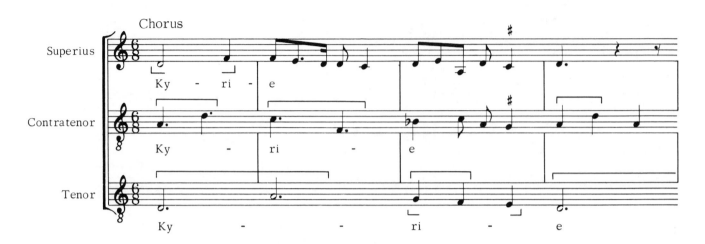

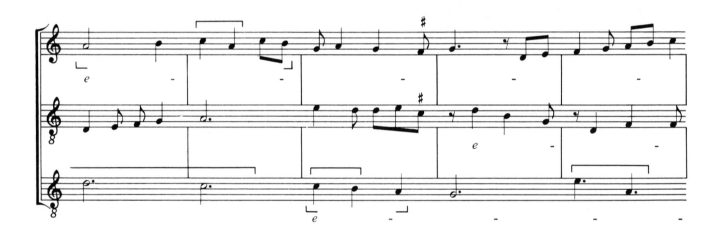

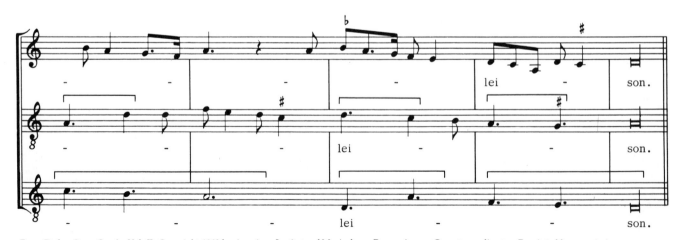

From Dufay *Opera Omnia*, Vol. II. Copyright 1960 by American Institute of Musicology, Rome, Armen Carpetyan, director. Reprinted by permission.
Engraving from *Music Literature: A Workbook for Analysis*, Vol. II by Hardy and Fish published by Harper & Row, Publishers, Inc.

Chorus

Lord have mercy

39 (to be prepared)
ADVANCED **CANON:** Entre vous, gentils amoureux
Guillaume Dufay

neus De bien ser - vir chas - cuns s'a - mi - e
jeux Et de me - ner tres bo - ne vi - e.
teus. Chan - tes, dan - ses, quoi que nul di - e;

l'an soy - es song - neus De bien ser - vir chas - cuns s'a - mi - e.
re ga - les et jeux Et de me - ner tres bo - ne vi - e.
lons et des - pi - teus. Chan - tes, dan - ses, quoi que nul di - e;

2. 8. Et de fu - ir me - ran - co - li - e,
6. Et qui ne puet chan - ter, se ri - e;

2. 8. Et de fu - ir me - ran - co - li - e,
6. Et qui ne puet chan - ter, se ri - e;

Se vous vo - les es - tre joi - eux.
Je ne vous ay con - si - lier mieux.

Se vous vo - les es - tre joi - eux.
Je ne vous ay con - si - lier mieux.

Between you, gentle lovers

1, 4, 7. Between you, gentle lovers,
this day of the year take care,
each of you, to serve well your friend.

2, 8.   And to shun sadness, if you would be happy.

3.   Seek only to cavort and play,
and to lead a very good life.

5.   And care not about the envious,
who are thieves and wretches.
Sing, dance, whatever anyone may say.

6.   And may he laugh who cannot sing;
I cannot give you better advice.

40

MODERATE

CHANSON: *Adieu m'amour et ma maistresse*
Gilles Binchois (c. 1400–1460)

1.4.7. A - dieu m'a - mour et ma mai - strais_____ se, _____
Fare - well my love and my dear la_____ dy, _____
3. J'ay grant de - sir de prendre a - dres_____ se, _____
Long - ing shall help me plan in se_____ cret, _____
5. Sou - ven - gne vous, bel - le de - es_____ se, _____
Do not for - get, O love - ly god_____ dess, _____

[CT]

[T]

A - dieu mon sou - ve_____
Fare - well my so - ve_____
Pour - quoy vous pui - se_____
How I may see you_____
De moy qui sui vo,_____
Your slave who serves you_____

rain_____ de_____ sir,
reign_____ de_____ sire,
re_____ ve_____ ir,
yet_____ a_____ gain,
sans_____ fail_____ lir,
with_____ out_____ fail,

2.8. A - dieu celle a_____ qui_____ veul_____ ser_____ vir,_____
Fare - well to her_____ whom_____ I_____ would_____ serve,_____
6. En vo - lon - te_____ de_____ re_____ ve_____ nir,_____
And in the thought_____ of_____ that_____ re_____ turn,_____

Farewell my love and my dear lady

41 **MASS:** *Sanctus*

Johannes Ockeghem (c. 1425–1495)

from the Missa prolationum

Holy Lord God Sabaoth.

FURTHER SUGGESTED STUDIES

1. Compose rhythmic exercises for class participation which utilize syncopation and shifting meters (from *duplum* to *triplum*). For example:

continue for at least nine measures

2. Bring additional examples to class from instrumental or vocal literature that pose rhythmic problems for performance. Solve the problems jointly by tapping and counting at sight.

Chapter 5
Sacred and Secular Music from the "Golden Age of Polyphony"

OBSERVATIONS

In several ways the sixteenth century is without parallel in the history of Western music. The gradual development of polyphony from the ninth century onward reached a zenith during this period of extraordinary activity in both sacred and secular music. The wide dissemination of Flemish music in the fifteenth century contributed to a uniformity of style in the sixteenth. A consummate technique was clearly evidenced by numerous composers. Liturgical music was typically tranquil and achieved, in masses and motets, a perfect complement to worship. Chordal style (also called *familiar style*), which encouraged congregational participation, was predominant in the Protestant Reformation service. In many compositions, however, both fugal and chordal textures were employed within the same work.

Secular music was at once abundant and lively. Poetic and dance forms guided structural premises; vernacular language was almost exclusively used; and major and minor tonalities became more clearly focused. A purely instrumental music was also highly esteemed, especially works for organ, virginal, and lute. "Singing with the lute" constituted a favored pastime and entertainment for both the amateur and professional (see Examples 66–68).

SUGGESTIONS

Chapter 5 contains accompanied solo songs; two-, three-, four-, and five-voice polyphony; and four-voice chordal examples.

1. It is suggested that the class be divided into small groups, with each one responsible for the preparation and class reading of specific works. Examples 42, 43, 45, 47, 48 and 50–55 will benefit from this kind of preparation. Examples 44, 46, and 49 should be read at sight by the entire class.
2. Voice majors may wish to prepare Examples 56–58 with the assistance of a keyboard instrument, lute, or guitar.
3. Although rhythmically easier than some previous examples, Example 43 contains the first instance of a "large triplet" (measure 2). Since the tempo is fast, it is suggested that the upper voice think two beats per measure while the lower voices think one beat per measure:

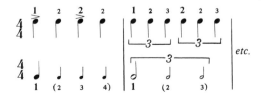

A *slow* tapping is recommended before attempting the fast tempo with text.

4. Example 55 illustrates a particular kind of text setting known as *vers mesurés*. The practice provides for a rhythmic setting that follows the declamation of the text, with the strong syllables twice the duration of the weak syllables. Variety in texture is achieved by the alternation of two-voice, three-voice, and four-voice settings. The composer was strongly influenced by literary models.

42 BASIC ENGLISH PART-SONG: A dew, a dew
Robert Cornysh (1465–1523)

43 MODERATE ENGLISH PART-SONG: I have been a foster
Robert Cooper (fl. 1530–1590)

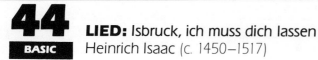

44
BASIC

LIED: *Isbruck, ich muss dich lassen*
Heinrich Isaac (c. 1450–1517)

45 TRACT: Ave Maria

MODERATE Heinrich Isaac

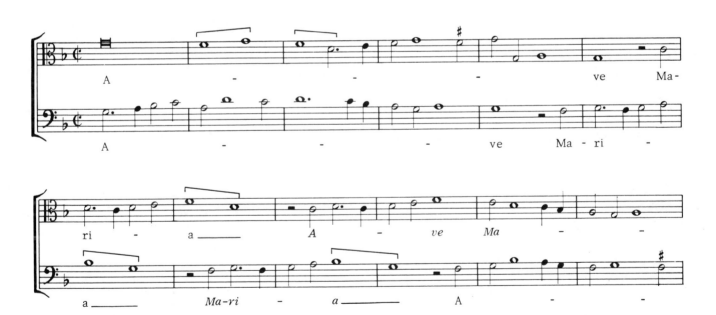

Engraving from *Music Literature: A Workbook for Analysis*, Vol. II by Hardy and Fish published by Harper & Row, Publishers, Inc.

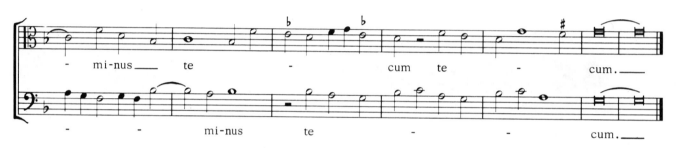

Hail Mary

Hail Mary full of Grace, the Lord is with thee.

*The bracket (⌐————⌐) indicates the presence in the original of a ligature, a symbol representing two or more successive notes.

MASS: Et incarnatus est

Josquin des Prez (1450–1521)

(from the Mass Pange Lingua)

And was incarnate

And (He) was incarnate by the Holy Ghost
of the Virgin Mary: and was made man.

MASS: Pleni sunt coeli

Josquin des Prez

from the Mass L'Homme armé

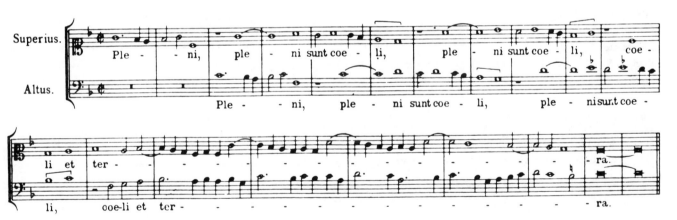

The Heavens are full

The heavens and the earth are full.

48
BASIC

MADRIGAL: Quando ritrova
Costanzo Festa (d. 1545)

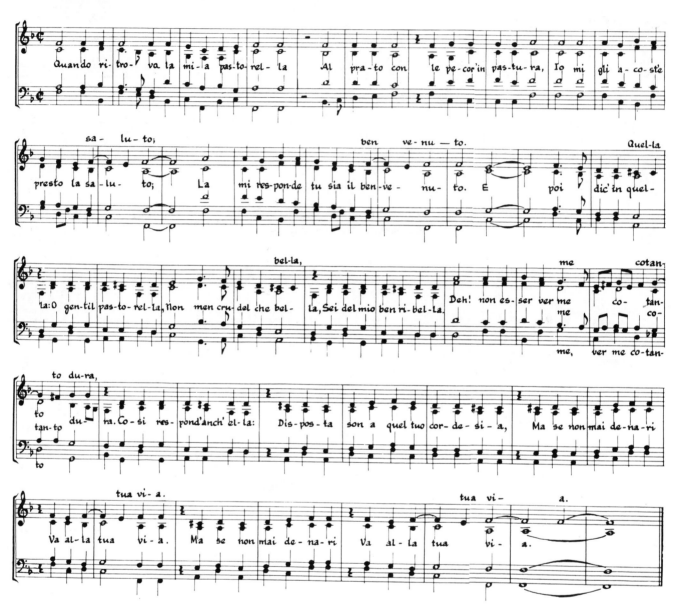

When I Meet

When I meet my shepherdess in the meadow, I approach and quickly greet her.
She answers, bidding me welcome. And then I tell her: Oh lovely shepherdess,
as cruel as you are pretty, you still reject my love. Come, do not be so cold with
me. And so she answers me: I like your courtesy, but if you have no money, go
on your way.

CHORALE: Aus tiefer Not
Johann Walter (1496–1570)

From deep despair

From deep despair I cry to you, Lord God, hear my calling.
For, if you will allow the sin and wrong that is done,
Who, Lord, can continue to be for you? Turn your merciful
ear to me and open it to my plea.

For, if you will allow . . . etc.

50 MODERATE

MOTET: *In manus tuas, Domine*
Thomas Tallis (c. 1505–1585)

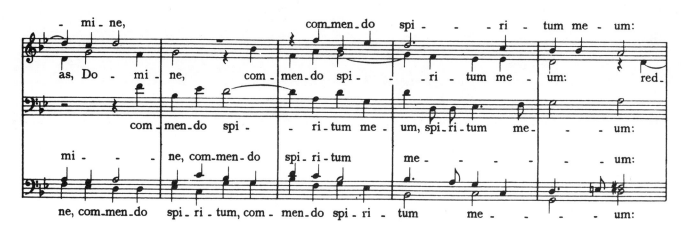

From *Geschichte der Musik in Beispielen* compiled and edited by Arnold Schering. Copyright © 1931 by Breitkopf & Härtel, Leipzig. Reprinted by permission of Broude Brothers Limited.

Into your hands, Lord

Into your hands, Lord, I commend my spirit. You have redeemed me, Lord, God of Truth, I commend my spirit.

51 **MODERATE** **MOTET:** *Ainsi qu'on oit le cerf bruire*
Claude Goudimel (c. 1510–1572)

From *Geschichte der Musik in Beispielen* compiled and edited by Arnold Schering. Copyright © 1931 by Breitkopf & Härtel, Leipzig. Reprinted by permission of Broude Brothers Limited.

As one hears the stag rustle

As one hears the stag rustle in pursuit of the cool waters,
Thus, Lord, my heart sighs for your streams, goes ever crying,
    following, the great living God.
Alas, when will that be,
that I will see the face of God?

52
ADVANCED

MOTET: *O magnum mysterium*
Tomás Luis de Victoria (c. 1549–1611)

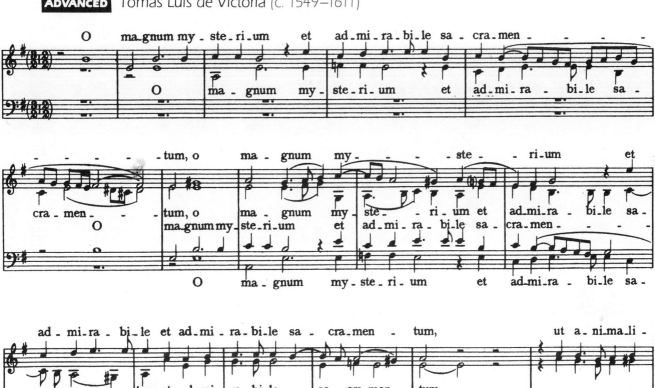

From *Geschichte der Musik in Beispielen* compiled and edited by Arnold Schering. Copyright © 1931 by Breitkopf & Härtel, Leipzig. Reprinted by permission of Broude Brothers Limited.

Oh great mystery

Oh great mystery and wondrous sacrament,
that the beasts should see the newborn Lord,
lying in the manger.

53
MODERATE

MASS: *Benedictus*
Giovanni Palestrina (c. 1525–1594)
from *Missa ad Fugam*

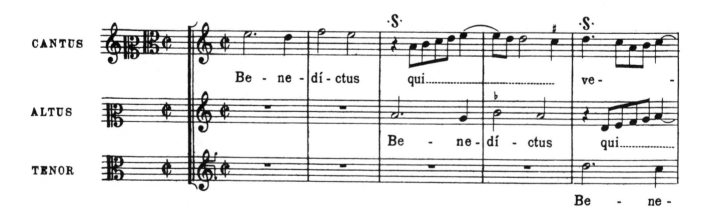

Blessed

Blessed is he who comes in the name of the Lord.

54

ADVANCED

(to be prepared)

MADRIGAL: *Ecco morirò dunque!*

Carlo Gesualdo (c. 1560–1613)

Lo! I shall die then!

Lo! I shall die then!
may you, who killed me with a look,
not see my dying.

55

CHANSON: O rôze reyne des fleurs
Claude Lejeune (1528–1602)

From *Geschichte der Musik in Beispielen* compiled and edited by Arnold Schering. Copyright © 1931 by Breitkopf & Härtel, Leipzig. Reprinted by permission of Broude Brothers Limited.

Chant à 4

Cet _ te bou _ che plei _ ne tou _ iours et d'o _ deur rar' et de dou _ ceur,

Et de son ris, et de son chant, et de son de _ vis si plai _ zant

Et de son bai _ zer a _ dou _ cit tou _ te l'ai _ greur que l'a _ mour fait.

O rose, queen of flowers

O rose, queen of flowers,
When I see you,
When I breathe your scent,
love holds me.

These lips of rare aroma and of sweetness,
With their smiles and song and charming chatter,
and with their kiss,
sweeten all bitterness that love imposes.

56 ACCOMPANIED SONG: Cantai un tempo

MODERATE Cosimo di Bottegari (1554–1620)

Can-tai un tem-po e se fu dolce il can-to Questo mi ta-ce-ro ch'al-tr'il sen-ti-va; Or è ben giunt'ogni mia fest' a ri-va Ed o-gni mio pia-cer ri-volt' in pian-to.

Once I sang

Once I sang, and if the song was sweet I shall not say, for another heard it;
Now all my joy has come to grief and my pleasure turned to tears.

Fortunate he who restrains desire and lives in repose:
Mine deprives me of peace and rest,
for I placed too much faith in another.

Wretch who hoped his love
would set a happy example
for the thousands who would follow.

Now I hope no longer,
and the depth of my pain shall be known to the world,
and to you, enemy of love and pity, and of mine.

57 ACCOMPANIED SONG: Ardo per mio destin

MODERATE

Cosimo di Bottegari

Published by Wellesley College in 1965. Reprinted by permission.

I burn for my destiny

I burn for my destiny and, at the same time, turn to ice;
I love who hates me, and who disdains me I honor,
and who flees me I follow and adore,
I spurn life and embrace my death.

Now I am free and now I find myself bound,
now I rejoice loving and now, rejoicing, die.
Now I am pleased, now slain by the great suffering,
now I detest, now crave the fierce impediments.

I weep, I laugh, and weary, abandon myself to the torments that yet make me so
    happy.
I hope, and fall into despair; am cheered, and saddened, by harsh fate.

Wretched I who has come to this,
that I wish I had never been born into this world!

58
BASIC

ACCOMPANIED SONG: *What if I never speed*
John Dowland (1563–1626)

Come, come, while I have a heart to de-sire thee, Come, come, come for ei-ther I will love or ad-mire thee.

FURTHER SUGGESTED STUDIES

1. As in the examples from Chapter 4, rhythm may pose greater problems than pitch. Devise rhythmic exercises in which the basic pulse shifts from measure to measure. For example, beat measures in one or two as indicated and select from a different rhythmic pattern each time:

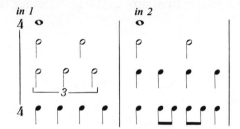

   This kind of exercise involves, of course, a thought process resulting in accurate temporal proportions rather than the intrusion of unwarranted mechanical accents within the phrase.

2. Too often, performers are precise with notes and neglect the accuracy of rests. Do you "play"/"sing" the rests with the same care and precision that you play/sing the notes? The note preceding the rest *must be held the full value.* An excellent class exercise is to have eight students each sing one note of a scale:

   What typically results is [rhythmic notation] indicating that the

full note value has not been observed.

PERFORMANCE SUGGESTIONS

The original manuscripts of notated music after about 1600 contain bar lines, placed by the composer for ease of reading by performers and to indicate consistent metrical groupings. The presence of bar lines, however, offers neither an invitation nor license to accent the first beat of each measure.

 Dance-derived music, whether vocal or instrumental, is typically more regular in rhythmic groupings, more constant in basic pulse, and may be—on occasion—more highly accented. *Song-derived* music (again, either instrumental or vocal or a combination of the two) is quite another matter. Song-derived music will tend to be less regular rhythmically, should contain some natural elasticity of phrases and periods, and will normally not be highly accented rhythmically. The accents will be achieved by high (pitch) points, dynamics, full textures, dissonance of pitches, etc.

Consider the following rhythmic line:

Such a disposition of accents is *possibly* appropriate for certain kinds of dance-derived music. Now consider the same line with a different disposition of accents:

A psychological accent (thought, not executed) on the fourth beat will propel the phrase, cause the greatest amount of tension to occur in measure 3, and will delineate more clearly the text (if any) and the musical structure as a whole. "Think last beat" should be a motto for the musical performance of *song-derived* literature. Further, the motto is appropriate for performance of such music from any century—whether the sixteenth, eighteenth, or twentieth.

Chapter 6
Diverse Examples from the Seventeenth Century

OBSERVATIONS

The Baroque era encompassed a 150-year period, approximately from 1600 to 1750, and produced several musical norms which are still utilized today. Standard notation was established; tonal music within a well-defined harmonic system was both discussed and composed; an independent and idiomatic instrumental style emerged.

Nuove musiche (new music) is a term used to describe early seventeenth-century music that seemed to initiate radical departures from the previous polyphonic era. Innovations included the use of dramatic declamation in music, called *recitative*, incorporated into new dramatic works (opera). A notational shorthand, termed *figured bass* (see Examples 59, 62) was widely used for the first time. Figured bass provided a clearly defined harmonic support for recitation, solo song, and other vocal and instrumental combinations (solo sonatas, trio sonatas, etc.).

Some composers, including Gesualdo in the late sixteenth century, employ a striking chromaticism. These "bent pitches" often relate to a heightened emotional level in setting such words as "sorrow" (lost love), "pain," "anguish," and "death." For the student of sight singing, this chromaticism will require special attention and tenacity in order to achieve perfection of intonation.

SUGGESTIONS

1. Since several of the examples in this chapter are for solo voice with lute or keyboard accompaniment, it is recommended that assignments be made to small groups of students.
2. Example 63 is one of the most demanding examples in the entire text.
   a. Begin preparation by carefully singing the chromatic scale several times:

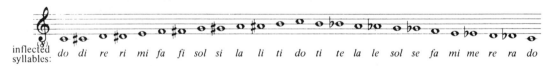

inflected syllables: *do di re ri mi fa fi sol si la li ti do ti te la le sol se fa mi me re ra do*

   (Tenors and basses: sing an octave lower than written.)
   b. Devise pitch exercises from the examples, to be sung many times—always checking intonation with a well-tuned instrument.

   c. Practice singing sixths.

3. Examples 61, 64, 65, and 67 should be sung at sight by the entire class. Examples 62 and 66 should be prepared in advance, paying particular attention to the rhythmic problems in both examples.

4. Examples 63 and 66 are constructed on a *ground* or *ground bass*. This procedure provides for several repetitions of a melodic bass line.

59 (to be prepared)
MADRIGAL: Dovrò dunque morire
MODERATE Giulio Caccini (c. 1560–1618)

60
MODERATE

(to be prepared)
MADRIGAL: Perchè se m'odiavi
Claudio Monteverdi (1567–1643)

Per - chè se m'o - dia - vi mo - stra - vi d'a - mar - mi mo -
Chi sa ch'u - na vol - ta la stol - ta fie - rez - za la
No no ohe non vo - glio se sco - glio m'a - spet - ta se

-stra - vi d'a - mar - mi per sol in - gan - nar - mi. Ahi, _____ stel - la ti
stol - ta fie - rez - za non bra - mi chi sprez - za. Ahi, _____ ch'i - o vo
sco - glio m'a - spet - ta driz - zar la bar - chet - ta. Più _____ fie - ra que-

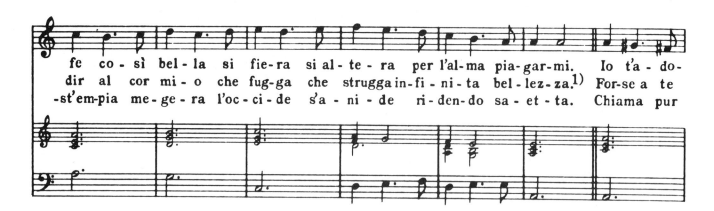

fe co - sì bel - la si fie - ra si al - te - ra per l'al - ma pia - gar - mi. Io t'a - do-
dir al cor mi - o che fug - ga che strug - ga in - fi - ni - ta bel - lez - za.[1] For - se a te
-st'em - pia me - ge - ra l'oc - ci - de s'a - ni - de ri - den - do sa - et - ta. Chiama pur

-ra-vo tu sprez-za-vi me em-pia Fil - li em-pia Fil - li per - chè?
toc-che-rà a chie-der pie-tà em-pia Fil - li em-pia Fil - li chi sa.
quan-to voi ch'io non ver-rò em-pia Fil - li em-pia Fil - li no no.

Why, if you hated me

Why if you hated me, did you show love for me, just to deceive me.

Oh, the stars made you so beautiful, proud, haughty to wound my soul.
I adored you, you spurned me, heatless Filli, why?

Who knows but that one day foolish pride will not crave what it spurned.

Oh, I will tell my heart to flee, to consume infinite beauty.
Perhaps it will be for you to beg mercy, heartless Filli, who knows.

No, I'll not, if rocks await me, steer the boat.
Fiercer arrow will find its mark, strike smiling this heartless vixen.

Call as you will I'll not come,
heartless Filli, no, no.

61 PSALM: Exultent caeli
Claudio Monteverdi

The heavens rejoice

Let the heavens rejoice and the angels be glad and let all people rejoice this day, sounding the instrument of gladness, the lutes, and the choirs.

62 (to be prepared)
MODERATE **RECITATIVE:** *Scorto da te*
Claudio Monteverdi
from *La Favola d'Orfeo,* Act III

ORFEO

Scor_to da te mio nu _ me Spe_ran_za, Spe_ran_za u_ni_co be_

_ne de gl'afflit _ ti mor_ta_ _li O_mai son giun_to

a questi me_sti e te_nebro_ si re_gni O_ve raggio di sol già mai non

Watched by you (from *The Fable of Orfeo*)

Watched by you, my god of hope,
  Hope, the only blessing of afflicted mortals,
I have arrived in this sad and shadowy realm
  where no ray of sun may penetrate.

You, my companion and guide on such strange
  and unknown paths, have directed the weak
  and trembling steps, so that even now I still hope
to see again those blessed lights (eyes)
  which alone give daylight to my eyes.

63 (to be prepared)
ARIA: Tremulo spirito
Pietro Francesco Cavalli (1602–1676)
Hecuba's lament

Po - ve - ro Pri - a - mo, scor - da - ti d'He - cu - ba, ve - do - va

mi - se - ra. Cau - sa - no l'ul - ti - mo

hor - ri - do e - si - li - o Pa - ri - de ed E - le - na.

Tremulous spirit

Tremulous spirit, weeping and weary, go quickly;
Fly, spirit, that turbid and greedy Erebus awaits.
Poor Priamus, forget Hecuba, forlorn widow:
Paris and Helen cause the final terrible exile.

NOTE: Examples 63 and 66 are constructed on a *ground* or *ground bass*. This procedure provides for several
repetitions of a melodic bass line.

64 BASIC

LIED: Viel schöner Blümelein
Johann Hermann Schein (1586–1630)

Many beautiful flowers

Many beautiful flowers have grown again in the cool May.
Of all those flowers, two please me: the longer-the-better,*
forget-me-not, etc.

*(honeysuckle)

65 BASIC

LIED: Gleich wie ein kleines Vögelein
Johann Hermann Schein

Just as the small bird

Just as the small bird, before it knows, is pitifully caught in the net, from which it cannot escape, but must ever remain prisoner.

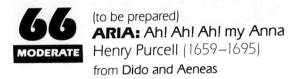

66 MODERATE

(to be prepared)
ARIA: Ah! Ah! Ah! my Anna
Henry Purcell (1659–1695)

from **Dido and Aeneas**

Ah! Ah! Ah! my An-na, I am

press'd With tor-ment, Ah! Ah! Ah! my An-na,

I am press'd With tor - ment not to be ex-press'd;

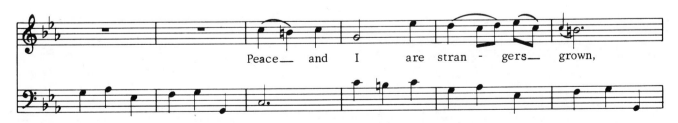

Peace and I are stran-gers grown,

From *Music Literature: A Workbook For Analysis*, Vol. II (pp. 43–45). Copyright © 1966 by Harper & Row, Publishers, Inc. Reprinted by permission of the publisher.

grown,   Peace___ and I are stran - gers,___ stran - gers___

Violino I

Violino II

Viola

grown.

Basso

67

MODERATE

ROUND: *I gave her cakes*
Henry Purcell

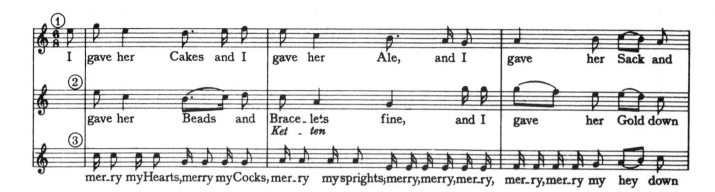

From *Geschichte der Musik in Beispielen* compiled and edited by Arnold Schering. Copyright © 1931 by Breitkopf & Härtel, Leipzig. Reprinted by permission of Broude Brothers Limited.

68

MODERATE

ROUND: Hark! Harry
John Eccles (c. 1650–1735)

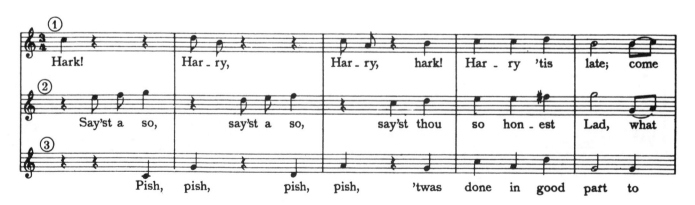

From *Geschichte der Musik in Beispielen* compiled and edited by Arnold Schering. Copyright © 1931 by Breitkopf & Härtel, Leipzig. Reprinted by permission of Broude Brothers Limited.

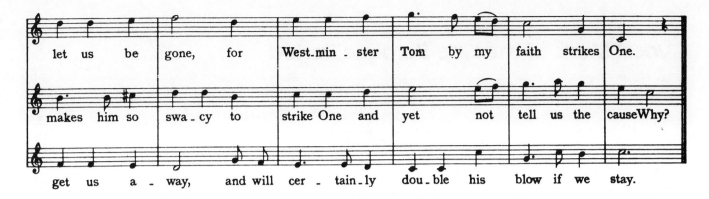

FURTHER SUGGESTED STUDIES

1. In addition to the exercises suggested at the beginning of this chapter, devise studies which drill on all intervals, e.g.:

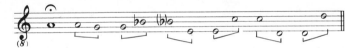

2. "Relative pitch" (as opposed to perfect pitch) *can* be developed. Suggest that an "a" be sung at the beginning of every class and that students attempt to sing an "a" several times daily—always checking accuracy with a pitch pipe or piano. A short exercise has been used with good results:

These are obviously "handy" pitches: the orchestra a', band b♭', and middle c' (all an octave lower for men).

Chapter 7
Vocal Music of the Late Baroque Period

OBSERVATIONS

A culmination of many styles and national traits was manifest in the first half of the eighteenth century—particularly as evidenced in the works of Bach and Handel, Couperin and Rameau. Generally speaking, forms were perfected and expanded rather than new ones invented. Tonal harmony became totally functional with a compelling musical logic; tonal counterpoint was fluid and technically perfect; imitation and sequence were the hallmarks of both the style and craft of many composers. The harmonic system typically involved a "gravitation pull" to the tonic, with the roots of preceding chords often being a perfect fifth or major second apart.

in C: iii vi ii V I I IV V I

Modulation (change of tonal levels) to closely related keys was a standard practice, effecting a rich but essentially diatonic vocabulary.

SUGGESTIONS

Examples 70–74 are in open score and use c clefs. C clefs were introduced in Chapters 1 and 3, but were not emphasized until this point in the text. The ability to read any of the seven clefs fluently is a requirement for the well-trained musician. The viola uses the alto clef, while bassoon, trombone, and cello employ the tenor clef on occasion. The principal advantages of clefs, however, are for the purposes of transposition. A few examples will illustrate:

1. It is recommended that each line of the Chorales (Examples 70–74) be read several times by the entire class, adjusting to an appropriate octave to accommodate range.

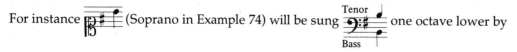

the tenors and two octaves lower by the basses. Similarly, the altos will find singing one octave lower more comfortable.

2. Example 77 may be read by the entire class or prepared by five soloists and accompanist for class presentation. Examples 76–79 will also serve well as individual or small group assignments.

3. In Example 79 a typical Baroque notational device is employed which denotes accented dissonants:

These embellishments should be performed as shown below:

These notes are *not* grace notes (♪) which are typically performed with a *very* short duration *before* the principal beat, and subtracted from the value of the previous beat.

69
MODERATE

MASS: Qui tollis
Johann Joseph Fux (1660–1741)
from *Missa canonica*

Thou who takest away

Thou who takest away the sins of the world, have mercy upon us.
Thou who takest away the sins of the world, receive our prayer.
Thou who sittest at the right hand of the Father, have mercy upon us.
Thou only are holy, Thou only art the Lord,
Thou only art most high, Jesus Christ.

70 MODERATE

CHORALE: *Christ lag in Todesbanden*
Johann Sebastian Bach (1665–1750)

Christ lay in the bonds of death

We eat and live well by the proper Easterbread, the old sour dough shall not
attend the word of Grace, Christ will be the sustenance and alone feed the soul,
faith wants no other life. Hallelujah!

Reprinted by permission of the publisher from *Chorales by Johann Sebastian Bach,* Book I, edited by Charles N. Boyd and Albert Riemenschneider.

71 MODERATE
CHORALE: Valet will ich dir geben
Johann Sebastian Bach

In mei-nes Her-zens Grun-de, dein Nam' und Kreuz al - lein Er-schein' mir in dem
Fun-kelt all-zeit und Stun-de, drauf kann ich fröh-lich sein.

Bil - de zu Trost in mei-ner Noth, wie du, Herr Christ, so mil - de dich hast ge-blut't zu Tod.

I will bid you farewell

In the depth of my heart your name and cross alone sparkle all time and hours,
of that I can be happy. Appear to me in the likeness to comfort me in my need, as
you, Lord Christ, so gently hast bled to death.

72 MODERATE
CHORALE: Vom Himmel hoch, da komm' ich her
Johann Sebastian Bach
from the *Christmas Oratorio*

Schaut hin! dort liegt im fin - stern Stall, dess' Herr-schaft ge - het ü - ber-all. Da

From Heaven on high I come

Look! There in the dark stable lies He whose dominion is over all. Where once a cow sought food, the Virgin's child now rests.

73

MODERATE

CHORALE: Ein' feste Burg ist unser Gott

Johann Sebastian Bach

Reprinted by permission of the publisher from *Chorales by Johann Sebastian Bach*, Book I, edited by Charles N. Boyd and Albert Riemenschneider.
Copyright © 1939 by G. Schirmer, Inc.

A mighty fortress is our God

They shall leave the word and have no thanks for it.
He surely is with us in the plan with His spirit and gifts.
If they take from us body, goods, honor, child and wife, let them go, there is no
    profit in them;
the Kingdom shall remain to us.

74

MODERATE

CHORALE: *Jesu, meine Freude*
Johann Sebastian Bach

Reprinted by permission of the publisher from *Chorales by Johann Sebastian Bach*, Book I, edited by Charles N. Boyd and Albert Riemenschneider.
Copyright © 1939 by G. Schirmer, Inc.

Jesus, my joy

Jesus, my joy, pasture of my heart, Jesus, my adornment, oh, how long the heart
is afraid and longs for you.
Lamb of God, my bridegroom, nothing on earth shall be dearer to me than you.

75 MASS: Et incarnatus est

ADVANCED

Johann Sebastian Bach
from the **Mass in B minor**

And was incarnate

And (He) was incarnate by the Holy Ghost of the Virgin Mary: And was made man.

76 (to be prepared)
RECITATIVE AND ARIA: Heroes, when with glory burning
George Frederick Handel. (1685–1759)

Now give the ar-my breath, let war a-while Smooth his rough

front, and wear a cheer-ful smile. The in-ter-val, if Ach-sah but ap-prove,

I'll con-se-crate to vir-tue and to love._

From *Alto Arias from Oratorios* compiled by Irving Brown. Copyright © 1977 by G. Schirmer, Inc. Reprinted by permission of the publisher.

77 (to be prepared)

Aria

From *Alto Arias from Oratorios* compiled by Irving Brown. Copyright © 1977 by G. Schirmer, Inc. Reprinted by permission of the publisher.

spirito

when with glo-ry burn-ing, All their toil with pleasure bear, And be-lieve, to love re-

p

cresc.

turn-ing, Laurel-wreaths beneath their care, lau-rel-wreaths be-neath their care.

cresc.

f

Dal Segno al Fine.

78 (to be prepared)
SONG: Doux liens
ADVANCED François Couperin (1668–1733)

[Con grazia; non troppo lento]

Doux li-ens de mon____ coeur, Ai-ma-bles pei-nes, Char-man-tes

chaî - - - - nes, De mo-ment en mo-ment Re-dou-

1. -blez mon tour-ment. 2. -ment. Un coeur ex-

-empt de nos ten - dres a - lar - mes Ne res - sen-tit ja-

Sweet charms

Sweet charms of my heart! beloved suffering! charming bonds! increase my torment at every moment. A heart which does not feel love's fears has felt only the smallest pleasure; for it is in his worst suffering that love has hidden his greatest pleasure.

79

(to be prepared)
RECITATIVE: Ma voix
Jean Philippe Rameau (1683–1764)
from *Castor et Pollux*

My voice (from *Castor and Pollux*)

My voice, mighty master of the world, lifts up trembling unto you. With a single look you dissipate my fear, calm also my profound anguish. Oh my father, hear my pleas! The immortality which enchains me is from now onward nothing but horrible torment for your son. Castor is no more, and my vengeance is vain if your sovereign voice does not call him back to happier days. Oh my father, hear my pleas!

FURTHER SUGGESTED STUDIES

Practice clef reading by reviewing Chapters 3–6. Substitute alto or tenor clefs and appropriate accidentals for transposing these melodies. Fluency is a requirement.

Chapter 8

Mostly Canons: Haydn, Mozart, Beethoven, and Schubert

OBSERVATIONS

The convergence of several diverse musical streams such as the French *style galant*, the North German "sensitive" style, Italian operatic traditions, and folk song imitations helped produce, between the approximate years 1750–1820, the amazing era called the Classical period. What it immediately calls to mind are the symphonies, string quartets, and keyboard works of the principal composers. Notable vocal/choral compositions include the operas of Mozart, the masses, oratorios, and operas of Haydn, and the monumental *Missa Solemnis* of Beethoven. Each composer also produced numerous songs and incidental vocal compositions—Schubert most prolifically among them. Schubert's songs, numbering more than 600, eloquently fuse German poetry with poignant lyric melody and provide a remarkable legacy of vocal literature. In all the music of this period, surface simplicity of melody, harmony, and rhythm was the norm. Textual contrasts, subtle colorations of timbre, balanced but slightly asymmetrical structures nevertheless resulted in a remarkably sophisticated product.

SUGGESTIONS

The Classical examples chosen for this text are somewhat atypical, with the exception of Examples 87, 88, and 95–97. Since the canons present few problems of pitch and rhythm, an additional opportunity to master the C clef is afforded.

1. Recommend that Example 81 be sung in at least five different keys, each version using a different set of clefs for each reading. Solfeggio systems may be profitably utilized; singing letter names may also be pedagogically beneficial.
   [Example 81]

2. Class performance of Example 95, with a discussion of phrasing, rubato, dynamics, diction, general performance practice of this late Classical/early Romantic song is encouraged.

80
BASIC

CANON: Tod und Schlaf
Franz Joseph Haydn (1732–1809)
Text: F. v. Logau

Tod ist ein lan - ger Schlaf, Schlaf ist ein
kur - zer, kur - zer Tod, die Not die lin-dert der und
je-ner tilgt die Not. Tod ist ein lan - ger Schlaf.

Death and sleep

Death is a long sleep, sleep is a brief, brief death. One softens misery, the other effaces it.

From Edition Peters 2965A. Reprint permission granted by C.F. Peters Corp., New York.

81
BASIC

CANON: Vixi
Franz Joseph Haydn

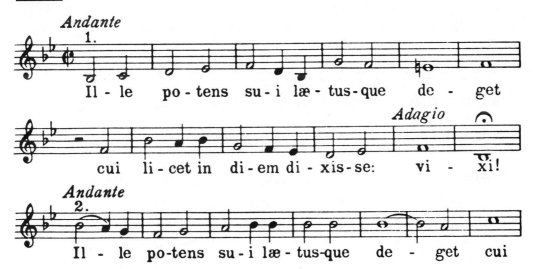

Il - le po - tens su - i læ-tus-que de - get
cui li - cet in di - em di - xis-se: vi - xi!
Il - le po-tens su - i læ-tus-que de - get cui

From Edition Peters 2965A. Reprint permission granted by C.F. Peters Corp., New York.

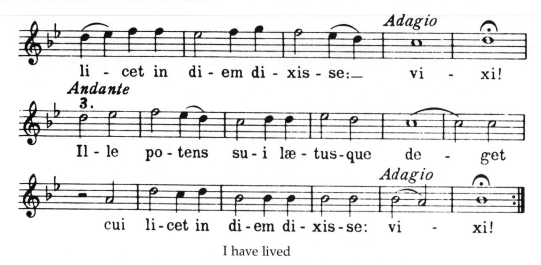

li - cet in di - em di - xis - se: vi - xi!

Il - le po - tens su - i læ - tus - que de - get

cui li - cet in di - em di - xis - se: vi - xi!

I have lived

That (time) will pass   Who can say to the day:
happily for him   I have lived!

82

CANON: Herr von Gänsewitz zu seinem Kammerdiener
Franz Joseph Haydn
Text: G. A. Bürger

Be - fehl doch, draußen still zu schwei - gen, ich

muß jetzt mei - nen Na - men schrei - ben, be - fehl doch

drau - ßen still zu schwei - gen, ich muß jetzt mei - nen

Na - men schrei - ben, ich muß, ich muß jetzt mei - nen

Na - men schreiben, schrei - ben, be - fehl doch still zu

From Edition Peters 2965A. Reprint permission granted by C.F. Peters Corp., New York.

schweigen, still zu schweigen, ich muß jetzt mein' Namen schreiben.

Sir Goosebrain to his valet

Give order that they be still outside,
now I must write my name, etc.

CANON: Vergebliches Glück
Franz Joseph Haydn
Text: Arabian proverb

Allegretto

Es ist um - sonst, daß dir das

Es ist um - sonst, daß

Glück. ge - wo - gen ist, wenn du nicht selbst er - kennst, wie

dir das Glück ge - wo - gen ist, wenn du nicht selbst er -

sehr du_ glück-lich bist. Es ist um -

kennst, wie sehr du_ glück-lich bist. Es

Vain luck

It is in vain, that luck be kind to you,
if you yourself do not recognize,
how happy you are.

84 CANON: Grabschrift
MODERATE
Franz Joseph Haydn
Text: P. W. Hensler

Hier liegt Hans Lau mit sei-ner Frau. Ein Hahn-rei war Hans

Lau, was war— denn, was war sei - ne Frau?

Epitaph

Here lies Hans Lau with his wife.
A cuckold was Hans Lau,
What, then, was his wife?

From Edition Peters 2965A. Reprint permission granted by C.F. Peters Corp., New York.

85 CANON: Thy voice o harmony
BASIC
Franz Joseph Haydn

*Each line can be performed four ways simultaneously as indicated by the printing of the text. Upon reaching the end of a line turn the music upside down (or right side up) and continue.

86-A
BASIC

MULTIPLE CANON: Erstes Gebot
Franz Joseph Haydn

Du sollst an ei - nen Gott glau - - ben.

First Commandment

Thou shalt believe in one God, etc.

86-B

A double crab canon   first part

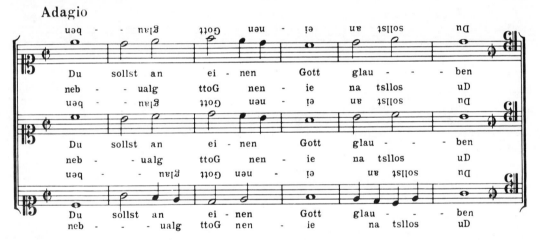

back
again
with the
new
notes

86-C

A four-way, three-voice canon

86-D

Du sollst an ei-nen Gott glau--ben

87
ADVANCED

(to be prepared)
MASS: Osanna in excelsis
Wolfgang Amadeus Mozart (1756–1791)
from *Requiem*

88 **ADVANCED** (to be prepared)
DUET: Bewahret euch
Wolfgang Amadeus Mozart
from *The Magic Flute*

Exeunt TWO PRIESTS.

What is their end? Des-pair and death.

What is their end? Des-pair and death.

89
MODERATE

CANON: *Ich bitt' dich*
Ludwig van Beethoven (1770–1827)

Sop. I

Ich bitt' dich, ich bitt' dich, schreib' mir die Es - Sca _ la auf.

Sop. II

Ich

Sop. III

A _____ bitt' dich, ich bitt' dich, schreib' mir die Es - Sca _ la auf.

A _____

Ich

From complete edition, vol. 29. Reprinted by permission of Belwin-Mills Publishing Corp.

For men: 𝄢♭♭♭♭ C

I beg you

I beg you, I beg you, write down the scale for me . . . etc.

90

MODERATE

CANON: Glück zum neuen Jahr
Ludwig van Beethoven

Happiness for the new year . . . etc.

91 MODERATE **RIDDLE CANON:** Si non per portas
Ludwig van Beethoven

Si non per por _ tas, per mu _ ros, per mu _ ros, per mu _ ros.

If not through the doors, then through the walls.

From complete edition, vol. 29. Reprinted by permission of Belwin-Mills Publishing Corp.

92 ADVANCED (to be prepared)
CANON: Lacrimoso son io
Franz Schubert (1797–1828)

MEN: transposed to c minor;
accidentals are shown

From *Franz Schubert—Complete Works.* Reprinted by permission of Dover Publications, Inc.

I am tearful . . . etc.

93 CANON: Gold'ner Schein

Franz Schubert

Text: Friedrich von Matthisson

Golden glow

Golden glow covers the forest, magic shimmer softly lights the ruins of the wooded Waldburg (Forest Castle).

94
MODERATE

CANON: Dreifach ist der Schritt der Zeit
Franz Schubert
Text: Friedrich von Schiller

From *Franz Schubert—Complete Works*. Reprinted by permission of Dover Publications, Inc.

Threefold is the tread of time

Threefold is the tread of time:
Hesitantly the future approaches,
Quick as an arrow the present flees,
Forever still stands the past . . . etc.

LIED: An den Tod
Franz Schubert
Text: C. F. D. Schubart

From *Franz Schubert—Complete Works.* Reprinted by permission of Dover Publications, Inc.

Death

Death, you terror of nature,
your clock ever trickles,
The swinging scythe glints,
grass and stalk and flower sinks.

Do not mow without distinction this flower,
just blossomed, this little rose, only half red,
be merciful, dear Death . . . etc.

Death, when will you come, my joy?
Draw the dagger from my breast?
Take the fetters from my hand?
Oh, when will you cover me with sand?
Come, oh death, if it please you,
fetch prisoners from the world:
come, end my misery,
be merciful, dear Death . . . etc.

MASS: Introit
Franz Schubert
Trans.: John Dressler

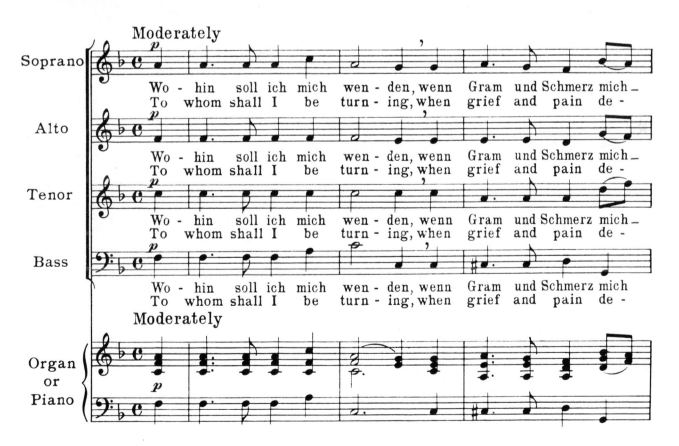

sen-dest ja die Freu-den, Du hei-lest je-den Schmerz.
Thou art send-ing rap-ture, Thou heal-est ev'-ry pain.

sen-dest ja die Freu-den, Du hei-lest je-den Schmerz.
Thou art send-ing rap-ture,Thou heal-est ev'-ry pain.

sen-dest ja die Freu-den, Du hei-lest je-den Schmerz.
Thou art send-ing rap-ture, Thou heal-est ev'-ry pain.

sen-dest ja die Freu-den, Du hei-lest je-den Schmerz.
Thou art send-ing rap-ture,Thou heal-est ev'-ry pain.

97

MODERATE

MASS: Benediction

Franz Schubert

Trans.: John Dressler

FURTHER SUGGESTED STUDIES

1. The easier slow movements of some of Haydn's string quartets provide excellent sight-reading materials. Instrumentalists may wish to bring such supplementary sources to class for this chapter.
2. Continue re-reading the earlier examples, changing the clefs to C clefs.

Chapter 9
Songs and Operatic Excerpts from the Nineteenth Century

OBSERVATIONS

Several critics writing during the nineteenth century considered melody to be the pre-eminent element, relegating harmony, rhythm, and the other parameters of music to a position of much lesser importance. There is little doubt that a beautiful, singable, even soulful series of pitches supported and enriched by a harmonic foundation represented the compositional goal of numerous composers of the Romantic era. It is not surprising, therefore, that solo song with piano accompaniment and opera are two of the most important genres of the century.

Melody became a subjective vehicle, the carrier of both emotion and message. Chromaticism was more widely employed than during the Classical period: Harmonies expanded from 7th and 9th chords through to the 13th—especially the dominant 13th chord; modulation was more frequent, often to distantly related keys or by means of enharmonic change. Rhythm was essentially "natural", i.e., supportive of speech patterns but, of course, involving *prolongation* in time. Prolongation is the slowing down and "stretching out" of speech patterns to achieve comprehensibility and a minimum of distortion within the tempo and mood set by the composer. The exception to this general principle of text setting is to be found in *recitativo secco* (literally, "dry reciting") which deliberately imitates spoken narrative. It is rapid, uses only a few different pitches, and typically has a minimal accompaniment.

The prolific output of poets and composers, together with their mutual esteem for each other, did produce an extraordinary wealth of German Lieder, French chansons, and English and American art songs during the period 1820–1900.

SUGGESTIONS

1. As in previous chapters, assignment of specific examples to individual students and/or small groups is desirable. *All* accompanied songs should be read or prepared at first *without accompaniment*. Solfeggio systems are appropriate for all, with the possible exception of Example 113, which will be very difficult with an inflected movable do system.
2. Examples 106–109 should be read at sight by the entire class.

98
BASIC

PART-SONG: Entflieh' mit mir, Op. 41 no. 1

Felix Mendelssohn (1809–1849)

Text: Heinrich Heine

Flee with me

Flee with me and be my wife, and rest by my heart; far away let my heart be your country and your home, far away . . . etc.

And if you do not flee I shall die here and you shall be lonely and alone; and even if you remain at home you'll be as though in a foreign land, and even if . . . etc.

From *Felix Mendelssohn—Songs for Voice and Piano,* Kalmus Study Scores #1214. Reprinted by permission of Belwin-Mills Publishing Corp.

99 PART-SONG: Es fiel ein Reif, Op. 41 no. 2

BASIC

Felix Mendelssohn
Text: Heinrich Heine

A frost fell

A frost fell in the spring night, fell on the colored flowers; they wilted, they dried up. A young man loved a maiden; they secretly fled from home, neither father nor mother knew. They wandered here and there, they found neither happiness nor luck; they died, they perished.

100

MODERATE

LIED: Du bist wie eine Blume, Op. 25, no. 24

Robert Schumann (1810–1856)

Text: Heinrich Heine

You are like a flower

You are like a flower, so beautiful, so pure, so kind;
I look at you and a sadness creeps into my heart.
I feel as though I should lay my hands upon your head,
praying that God may keep you, so beautiful, so pure, so kind.

101 MODERATE

LIED: Ich grolle nicht, Op. 48 no. 7
Robert Schumann
Text: Heinrich Heine

Nicht zu schnell *(not too fast)*

Ich grol - le nicht, und wenn das Herz_____ auch bricht,

e - wig ver - lor' - nes Lieb, e - wig ver - lor' - nes Lieb!_____ ich

I do not rage

I do not rage, even if my heart breaks. Love, lost forever, I do not rage! However you may radiate in diamond splendor, no ray falls into your heart's night, I've long known that. I do not rage, even if my heart breaks. I saw you in my dream, and saw the night in your heart, and saw the snake that eats at your heart, I saw, my love, how great your misery. I do not rage.

102 MODERATE

LIED: Schmerzen
Richard Wagner (1813–1883)
Text: Mathilde Wesendonck
Trans.: Grace Hall

Langsam und breit
Adagio ben sostenuto

Son - ne, wei-nest je-den A-bend dir die
Ev - 'ry eve-ning at thy set-ting Red thine

schö-nen Au - gen roth, wenn im Mee-res-spie - gel ba-dend dich er-reicht der frü - he
eyes are, lord - ly Sun, As in - to the sea thou sink-est Weep-ing, thy day's jour-ney

Tod; doch er-steh'st in al - ter Pracht, Glo - ri - e der düst-ren Welt, du am
done; Yet the morn-ing sees thee rise Glo - rious from the dusk - y deep, Proud e-

mit grosser Steigerung
crescendo molto

Und ge - bie - ret Tod nur Le - ben, ge - ben Schmer - zen Won - nen
For if death en - gen - ders liv - ing, And new hopes are born of

cresc.

molto rit. *a tempo*

nur: O wie dank' ich, dass ge - ge - ben sol - che
fears, Then may we give thanks to Na - ture For the

ff molto rit. *a tempo* *p* *cresc.*

Schmer - zen mir Na - tur!
boon of pain and tears!

f *f*

rit.

p *f* *p a tempo* *cresc.* *ff* *dim.* *p*

103
ADVANCED

RECITATIVE: O tu che sei d'Osiride
Giuseppe Verdi 1813–1901
from *Aida*

High Priestess.

(From a boat which approaches the shore descend Amneris and Ramphis, followed by some women closely veiled. Guards.)

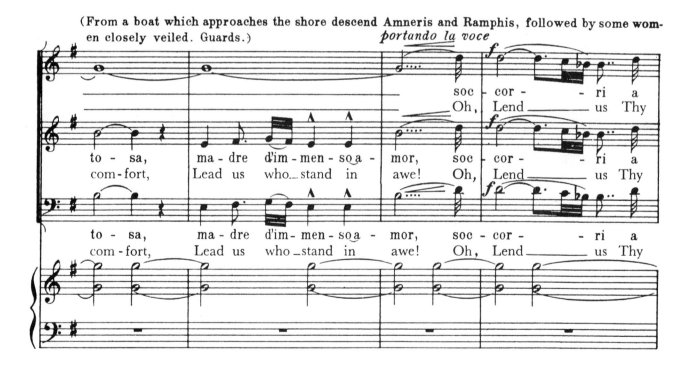

104
MODERATE

LIED: Mit einer Primulaveris, Op. 26 no. 4

Edvard Grieg 1843–1907
Text: J. Paulsen
English: F. Carder
German: W. Henzen

Allegretto dolcissimo

beau - ti - ful   is   sum - mer - time,   the
vist er Som - ren lys og smuk og

au - tumn cheers your heart,_____ but spring is yet the
rig___ er Li - vets Höst,_____ men Vå - ren er den

love - li - est when sweet - hearts nev - er   part._____ For
dej - lig - ste med El - skovs Leg___ og Lyst._____ Og

poco rit.

pp

You beautiful child of spring

105

MODERATE

LIED: Auf ein altes Bild
Hugo Wolf (1860–1903)
Text: Eduard Mörike
Trans.: H. Cecil Condrey

Langsam *(Slowly)*

In

grü - ner Land-schaft Som - mer - flor, bei küh - lem Was - ser,

Schilf und Rohr,__ schau, wie das Knäb - lein sün - de - los, frei__

106
MODERATE

PART-SONG: Ich schwing mein Horn ins Jammertal, Op. 41 no. 1
Johannes Brahms (1835–1897)

I turn my horn to the vale of misery

1. I turn my horn to the vale of misery, my joy has vanished; I was hunting, but must desist, the game runs before the hounds. A noble beast I had chosen from this field; it left me, as I well know, my hunting days are over.

2. Go on, wild game, to forest's pleasure, I shall not frighten you again by hunting your snow-white breast; another shall awaken you with hunter's cry and dog's bite so that you'll not escape; take care, my good beast! With sorrow I say farewell.

3. No big game can I capture, for this I often suffer; yet still I follow the hunter's trail, although luck comes rarely. If beautiful big game is not my due, I shall content myself with rabbit meat, it shall not sadden me.

107

CANON: Göttlicher Morpheus, Op. 113 no. 1

Johannes Brahms

Text: J. W. von Goethe

Divine Morpheus

Divine morpheus, in vain you wave the lovely poppies; the eyes still remain
open if Amor does not close them for me.

CANON: Wann? Op. 113
Johannes Brahms
Text: Ludwig Uhland

When?

When? When will heaven stop punishing (me) with albums and autographs?
When?

109

MODERATE

CANON: Spruch, Op. 113
Johannes Brahms
Text: Hoffmann von Fallersleben

Verse

In this world of deceit and pretense may God protect you, that the virginal beautiful flower of your being never be dimmed.

110

MODERATE

LIED: Morgen, Op. 27 no. 4
Richard Strauss, 1884–1949
Text: J. H. Mackay
English: John Bernhoff

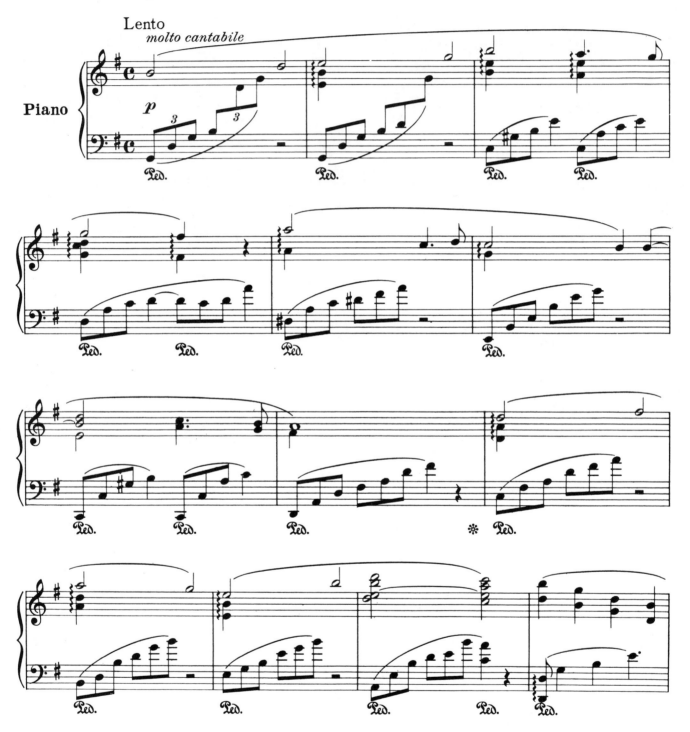

SONG: A Dissonance
Alexander Borodin (1833–1887)
Text: Alexander Borodin
English: Kurt Schindler

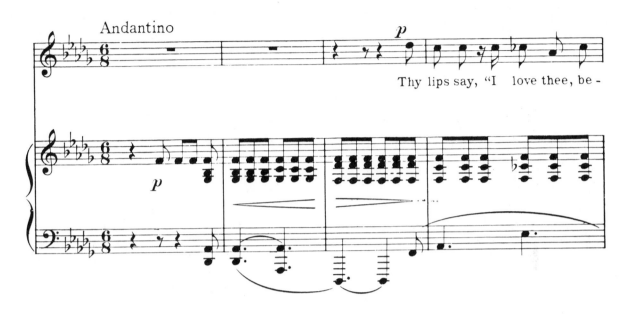

Thy lips say, "I love thee, be-

lieve me;"   And yet,   in the sound of thy

112

MODERATE

SONG: Lydia, Op. 4 no. 2
Gabriel Fauré (1845–1924)
Text: Leconte de Lisle
English: Marion Farquhar

Le jour qui lui est le meil-leur, Ou-bli-ons l'é - ter-nel-le tom - be,
This day is bright with no e - clipse, Soon the tomb brings e-ter-nal slum - ber,

Lais-se tes bai-sers, tes bais - sers de_ co - lom - be Chan-ter sur ta lèvre en fleur,
Then like the dove, let your kiss-es with - out num - ber, Sing_ on your bloom-ing lips,

sur ta lèvre en fleur. Un lys ca-ché ré -
on your bloom - ing lips. A hid-den flow'r with -

pand sans ces - se Une o - deur di - vine en ton sein;
out ces-sa - tion Breathes the sweet per-fume of your heart;

113

(to be prepared)
SONG: Beau soir
Claude Debussy (1862–1918)
Text: Paul Bourget
English: Henry G. Chapman

Andante ma non troppo

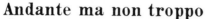

Lorsque au so-leil cou-chant les ri - viè - res sont

ro - ses, Et qu'un tiè - de fris - son court sur les champs de

114

ADVANCED

(to be prepared)
RECITATIVE: Non ditemi nulla
Giacomo Puccini (1858–1924)
from Madame butterfly

FURTHER SUGGESTED STUDIES

1. Devise solfeggio studies based on 7th chords and altered chords. For example:

In C major: (inflected)   do   mi   sol   ti   te   sol   mi   di   re   fa   le   do   do   la   fi   re   sol   ti   do   do

2. Practice singing secondary leading tones in both the major and minor scales. For example:

In C major: do   si   la   fi   sol   ri   mi   ti   do

In A major: do   do   sol   le   fi   sol   mi   fa   di   re   ti   do

Chapter 10
Vocal Music from the Twentieth Century: 1900–1950

OBSERVATIONS

A cyclic view of history gains credibility when considering the development of Western music. Every three hundred years composers have seemingly advocated radical changes and departures from existing conventions and mannerisms of previous periods. The *Ars Nova* of 1300, the *Nuove Musiche* of 1600, and the "new music" of 1900 all shared certain proclivities: an extensive examination, expansion, and modification of rhythm, pitch and simultaneity.

In the twentieth century, dissonance became a relative and subjective auditory factor, as opposed to a theoretical concept and set of norms. Thus melody and harmony were emancipated from the major-minor tonal system that evolved from the seventeenth century onward. Similarly, the bar line (often considered "tyrannical") was either omitted or forced into a new role which permitted free rhythms, non-regular groupings, and asymmetrical phrases.

Melody freely used all twelve notes of the chromatic scale, either in a systematized fashion (12-tone method) or, more subjectively, in a style of free or total chromaticism. The triad was often replaced by quartal harmonies, mixed chromatic harmonies, or non-classified "complexes" derived from serial techniques.

Unlike the accompaniments in many of the nineteenth-century songs which conveniently doubled the voice part, twentieth-century accompaniments frequently provide a different dimension of sound. Occasionally, accompaniments seem scarcely related to the vocal line; at other times the student will find them distracting or even antagonistic. The problems will be worth solving, however, not only for the musical results but also for the attainment of a sharpened and decisive musicianship.

SUGGESTIONS

1. Most of these twentieth-century examples will require a mastery of intervals, both simple and compound. Therefore, interval drills should be reviewed and intensified. It is recommended that the writing out and singing of a series such as M6–m2–A4–M7–etc. be a part of each day's technical studies.
2. Analyze the examples for comparison to known patterns or familiar scales. For instance, Example 115 looks difficult, yet becomes very readable after analysis:

3. Compound intervals can be mastered quite rapidly by intensive drill. The difficult

   interval [musical notation] becomes manageable when the octave is first sung aloud,

   then "sung" silently: [musical notation]
   sing   *think*

4. Rhythmic drills should be extrapolated from Example 123, while conducting drills involving meter changes are appropriate for Example 126:

$$\frac{3}{4} \quad \frac{2}{4} \quad \frac{3}{4} \quad \frac{4}{2} \quad \frac{3}{4} \quad \frac{3}{2} \quad \frac{3}{4} \quad \frac{2}{4}$$

$$\frac{3}{2} \quad \frac{2}{4} \quad \frac{2}{2} \quad \frac{2}{4} \quad \frac{3}{4} \quad \frac{3}{2} \quad \frac{3}{4} \quad \text{etc.}$$

115 (to be prepared)
SONG: The Cage
Charles Ives (1874–1954)
Text: Charles Ives

ADVANCED

NOTE:- All notes not marked with sharp or flat are natural.

SONG: Like a sick eagle

(to be prepared)

Charles Ives

Text: John Keats

I must die, like a sick ea-gle look-ing towards the sky.

117
ADVANCED

SONG: Der Tod
Anton von Webern (1883–1945)
Text: Matthias Claudius

Voll schmerzlicher Trauer

Ach, es ist so dun-kel in des To - des Kam-mer,

tönt so trau - rig, wenn er sich be-wegt und nun auf-hebt sei - nen

schwe-ren Ham-mer   und die Stun-de schlägt.

Death

Ah, it is so dark in Death's chamber;   And now lifts up his heavy hammer
It sounds so mournful when he stirs   And the hour strikes.

118 BASIC

SONG: Der Mai tritt ein mit Freuden
Arnold Schönberg (1874–1951)
pre-1545 folk song

Nicht langsam (♩ = 120)

1. Der   Mai   tritt   ein   mit
ed - les   Rös - lein
Sil - ber   und   rot
Rös - lein,   sei   mein

Freu - -den,   hin - fährt der Win - ter   kalt;   die
zar - -te   von   ro - ten Far - ben   schön   bin
Gol - -de   für   Per - len, E - del - stein   bin
We - ge - wart,   freund - li - chen ich   dich   bitt;   mein

May comes in with pleasure

1. May comes in with pleasure,
   cold winter goes away;
   the flowers in the meadow
   bloom in profusion.

2. A tender noble rose, of beautiful red hue,
   blooms in the garden of my heart;
   I crown it for all flowers.

3. More than silver and bright gold,
   than pearls and precious stones,
   I cherish the little rose:
   nothing is dearer to me.

4. Oh, little rose, be my guide,
   I beg you kindly;
   my elder-stick for all the way, and
   too, forget me not!

119
ADVANCED

(to be prepared)
SONG: (Tears of autumn), Op. 16 no. 1
Béla Bartók, (1881–1945)
English: Willis Wager

120
MODERATE

SONG: Chanson du clair tamis
Francis Poulenc (1899–1963)
Text: Maurice Fombeure
English: Winifred Radford
from **Chansons villageoises**

SONG OF THE CLEAR TAMIS

121

ADVANCED

(to be prepared)

CHORUS: God, the Lord shall be my light
Arthur Honegger (1892–1955)
from *Le Roi David*

122
ADVANCED

(to be prepared)
CHORUS: Thus spake Isaiah
William Walton
from *Belshazzar's feast*

123

MODERATE

CHORUS: Fortune plango vulnera
Carl Orff (b. 1895)
from *Carmina burana*

I deplore my wounds

1. I deplore my wounds with weeping eyes,
   because rebellious Fortune withdraws her
      gifts from me.
   It is true that, while opportunity with a
      hairy head is chosen,
   for the most part one with a bald head follows.

2. On Fortune's throne I had sat exalted,
   Crowned by the changing flower of prosperity;
   I indeed, who blossomed happy and blessed,
   have now fallen, deprived of glory,
      from the height.

3. The wheel of Fortune is turned: I fall diminished;
   Another is raised on high; the king sits exceedingly
      exalted at the summit, let him beware ruin!
   For beneath the heavens we behold Hecuba the queen.

124

PART-SONG: Un cygne
Paul Hindemith (1895–1963)
Text: Rainer Maria Rilke
from Six chansons

A swan

A swan advanced on the water,
   Quite surrounded by himself,
Like a gliding picture.

Thus, at certain moments,
   A being that one loves
Is [seen as] a moving space.

It draws near, doubled,
   Like this swan that swims
Before our troubled soul,

Which adds to that being
   The trembling image
Of happiness and doubt.

125 **ADVANCED**

LULLABY: Mädel, was fangst Du jetzt an?
Alban Berg 1885–1935
from *Wozzeck*

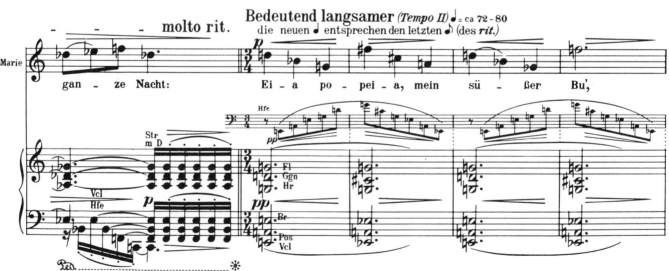

*) Das neue ♩. entspricht dem letzten (ritardierten) ♩ des 3/4 Takts.

Lullaby: Girl, what will you do

(Marie):   Girl, what will you do? You have a child
and no husband! Oh, no point in asking,
I'll just sing all night: Lullaby, my sweet
boy, no one cares a whit.

Johnny, hitch the six white horses, give
them food again. They won't eat oats,
they'll drink no water—
nothing but a lot of cool wine!
nothing but a lot of cool wine!

126

(to be prepared)
CANTATA: excerpt
Anton Webern (1883–1945)
from Kantate I*

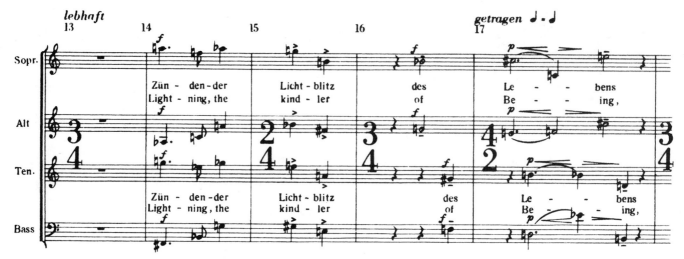

*Instrumental parts omitted here.

FURTHER SUGGESTED STUDIES

The student may wish to investigate the exercises in the following books for supplementary materials:

Paul Hindemith, *Elementary Training for the Musician*. New York: Associated Music Publishers, 1948.
Lars Edlund, *Modus Novus*, Nordska Musikvorlag, Stockholm, 1968.

Chapter 11
Music Since 1950

OBSERVATIONS

The experimental nature of the music of the 1950s and early 1960s imposed extraordinary technical demands on singers and instrumentalists alike. The post-Webern era ranged from total serialization (i.e., pre-determined pitch, duration, dynamics, articulation, etc.) to nearly total freedom in certain aleatoric works. Improvisation became a necessity as performer joined composer in the creation of new works—that were different at each "performance" (David Tudor playing John Cage, for example). A superb rhythmical technique is a prime requirement for numerous works of Boulez (*Le Marteau sans Maître*), Berio (*Sequenza*), Carter (*Double Concerto*), and Stockhausen (*Klavierstücke*). As Olivier Messiaen suggested in discussing harmony, "We had hit the ceiling." Since the parameters of pitch and their combinations seemed worn and often tired, rhythm, meter, mobility and flux versus stasis, texture and timbre, events involving audience participation—all became areas of exploration and development.

During the 1970s, however, a considerable synthesis has evolved which incorporates, combines, and distills several of the divergent and experimental exponents of the preceding fifteen years. There is no question whatever that the twentieth century has stretched each element of music, found new drama in both the dissonance and the consonance, has required a new dimension of technical skill from all practitioners and, hopefully, has added intellectual and emotional stimulation for the listener.

SUGGESTIONS

1. Examples 127 and 128 can be read at sight. Instrumental accompaniment for Example 128 is strongly recommended.
2. Example 130 will require preparation. Technical studies devised from short fragments of this song (see Chapter 10) will be beneficial. It is advisable to separate rhythmic problems from pitch problems in initial studies.
3. Example 134 is perhaps one of the most eloquent examples of twentieth-century literature. A prepared class performance will not only be technically challenging and rewarding, but may also yield many converts to the music of our time.

ROUND: Love is a circle
Ross Lee Finney (b. 1906)
from Spherical madrigals

128 CANTATA (excerpt): A lyke-wake dirge

Igor Stravinsky 1882–1971

from Cantata

129

MODERATE

SONG: Dreaming of a dead lady
Lennox Berkeley (b. 1908)
Text: Shên-Yo
Trans.: Arthur Waley
from **Five chinese songs**

130
ADVANCED

(to be prepared)
SONG: Tre poemi (I)*
Luigi Dallapiccola 1901–1976
Italian version: Eugenio Montale

*Only the vocal part and the piano reduction are shown here.

-vi - glia___ che ve-li ne'tuoi oc - chi, o__ mi-a az - zur - - - - ro-ve-na-ta fi - glia.___

Delicate white rose and frail fingers
of her who offered it,
of her whose soul is paler and more wan
than the faded wave of time.

Fragile and beautiful as the rose and even more fragile
is the strange marvel
you veil in your eyes,
oh my azure-veined daughter.

131
BASIC

SONG: Forbidden fruit
Gerald Warfield (b. 1940)
Text: Emily Dickinson

For - bid-den fruit___ a fla-vor has That law-ful or-chards mock;

How lus-cious lies the pea with - in the pod that du - ty locks.___

132 **CANON:** Signpost I
Eskil Hemberg (b. 1938)
from Signposts

Tenori Bassi

Soprani Contralti

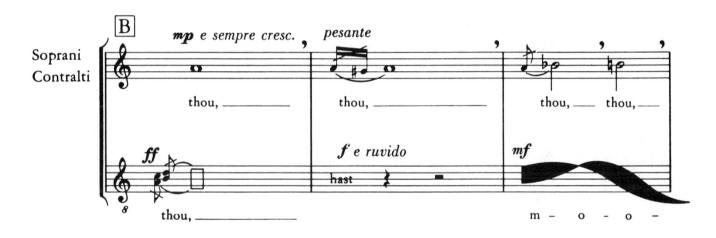

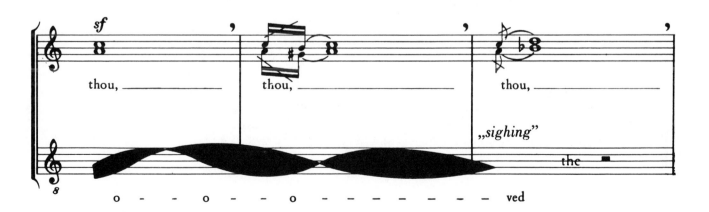

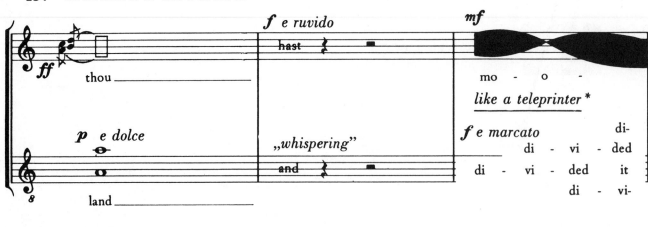

*Teleprinter passage moves 4 times faster than tempo

133

ADVANCED

CHORUS: Signpost II
Eskil Hemberg
from Signposts

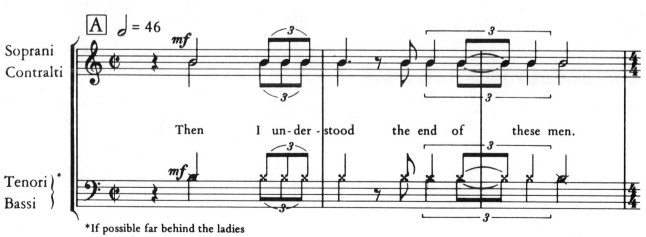

*If possible far behind the ladies

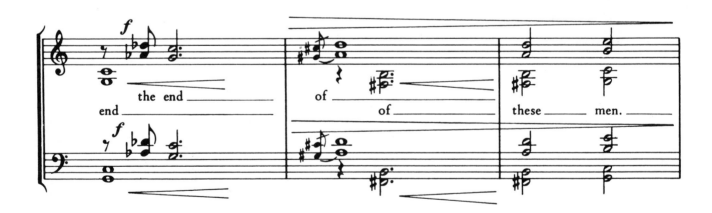

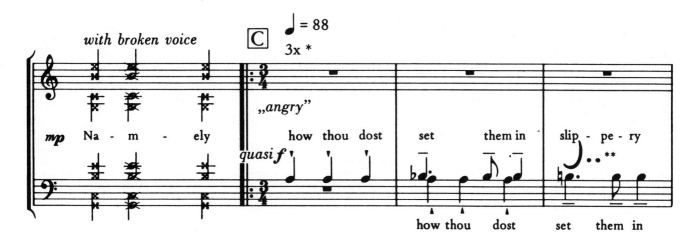

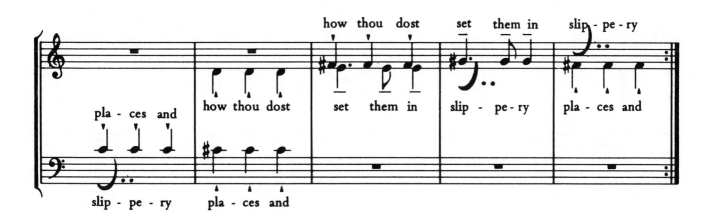

*Repeat this passage three times, each time a semitone higher

**Free and non-rhythmic!

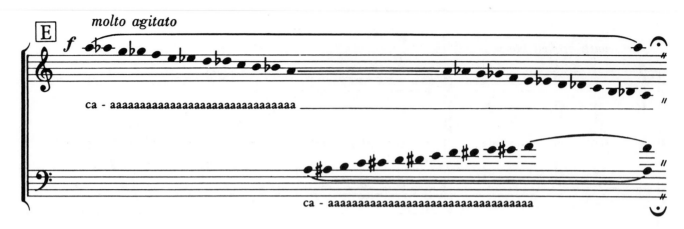

134

ADVANCED

SONG: Each afternoon in Granada, a child dies each afternoon
George Crumb (b. 1928)
Text: Garcia Lorca
from *Ancient voices of children*

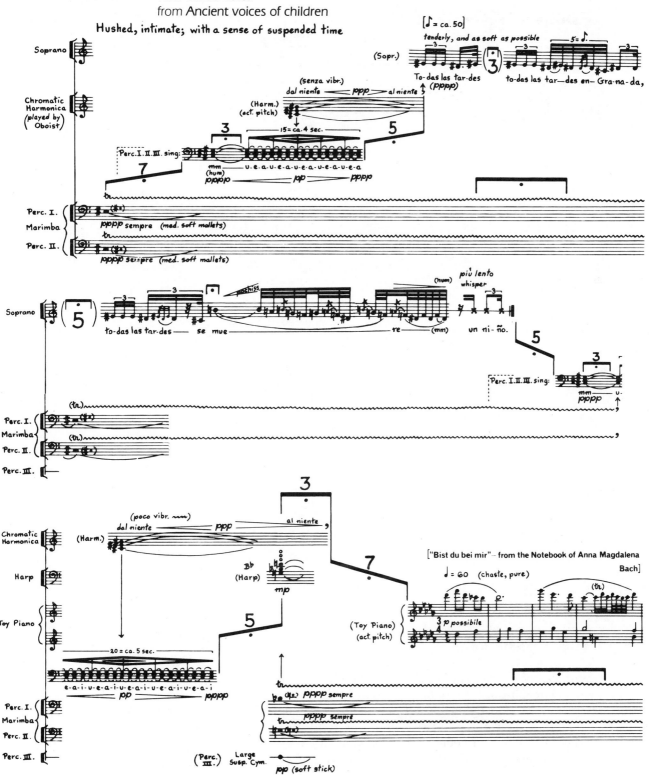

FURTHER SUGGESTED STUDIES

These examples of great vocal literature can provide a basic introduction to Western music—not by reading about it or listening to it but by singing it.

It is strongly recommended that a review of the preceding eleven chapters be undertaken periodically, singing one or two examples from each chapter. Each successive reading should produce refinements of intonation, rhythmic accuracy, clearly defined phrasing and cadencing, and a greater depth of understanding of the music.

PART TWO
Folk Songs

The oral traditions of folk music present diverse problems for the scholarly collector, the music publisher, and the student of sight singing. A very popular melody will exist in numerous versions. Variations of the basic melody are common, including embellishment as well as changes in the rhythmic and metric features. Similarly, the text may contain minor differences from version to version or indeed may tell an entirely different story—adapted, of course, to the locale, time, interests, and perhaps social needs of the narrators. The perceptive music student will find the study of folk music both challenging and musically rewarding.

Part Two has four divisions, each unified by pitch content—i.e., the *scale* that determines the tonal basis of the songs. Examples 134–156 are based on the major scale with very few alterations, 157–165 on the minor scales, 166–177 on modal inflections, and 178–190 are of mixed pitch resources. It should be noted that the basic criteria for melodies in the minor mode are the presence of the minor third from the tonic and the *raised* leading tone. Therefore some melodies in the modal division are actually tunes which utilize the natural or "pure" minor scale. Within each division a modest attempt has been made to order the materials from technically easy to more complex.

Language glossaries in Latin, French, German, and Italian are included in the appendix as an aid to those students studying one of the languages and as a guide for voice, conducting, history, composition, and theory majors in particular. The folk songs of Part Two are from many countries; glossaries for these diverse languages are beyond the scope of this text. Solfeggio systems and English translations are entirely appropriate for these songs.

Folk songs of the past and the best of the popular tunes of today serve as a catalogue of people's interests, moods, aspirations, and despairs. History, legend, and myth are interwoven and spun out. The bard of antiquity and the present decade's singer of social commentary share a common lineage. Several compilers of folk songs (for example John and Alan Lomax) classify their collections by locale or purpose: sea chanties, historical ballads, work and social songs, those with religious texts, love lyrics, etc.

For practical reasons, several texts have been confined to one or two verses. However, complete lyrics are included in sufficient number to provide the student with considerable insight into the folklore of Western civilization. It is a rich source of information and a fascinating study in symbolism. The apparent surface naiveté of many of the texts is often misleading: they may well contain several layers of meaning—the obvious literal one, of course, but also perhaps one of religious connotation, or of very worldly, physical allusion, or of contemporary political and social satire. Gertrude Stein's fabled line "A rose is a rose is a rose . . ." does not quite apply, in its literal sense, to folklore. A white rose, for instance, may well refer to the flower, but also to the Virgin Mary, or to a maiden being ardently pursued by her lover, or perhaps to the Wars of the Roses in fifteenth-century Britain.

Some folk melodies, especially those from Slavic countries and from Greece, are quite difficult in terms of both rhythm and interval content. These will require preparation and great attention to accuracy of durations and pitches.

Chapter 12
Folk Songs in Major Keys

SUGGESTIONS

Both fixed do and movable do solfeggio systems are appropriate for the melodies in Chapter 12. The first reading should be rhythmically strict. After the melody has been learned, however, it is suggested that the metronomic precision be relaxed in favor of a logical and natural presentation of the text.

Accompaniment chords are suggested.* Piano, guitar, harp, vibes are possibilities—after the melody has been learned. Exercises should be devised for accuracy of pitch and intonation. For example:

1.
G major
movable *do*:   sol   do   do   sol   mi   mi   sol   sol   sol

2.
a minor
movable *do*:   do   sol   la   ti   do   te   le   sol

Patterns should become instinctive. For example:

3.
fixed or movable *do*:   do   fa   mi   do   la   sol   do   ti   do
movable inflected *do*:   do   fa   me   do   le   sol   do   te   do

*In many cases, the chord suggestions by the editor of the collections from which these folk songs are taken have been retained. These letters (see Ex. 135: G A D C D etc.) are to be used as a general guide for harmonization. Alternative harmonizations are encouraged; for example 135, measures 1–6, might lend itself appropriately to the following:

1	2	3	4	5	6	
G Maj	e min	a min	D Maj	G Maj	C₆ Maj	D Maj

135

The cool, sweet water
(Išla Děvečka)
Czechoslovakia

1 Down by the lakeside
Fetching the water
One fine day,
I heard a young girl,
Sent by her mother,
Softly say:

2 Clear running water,
So sweet and cooling,
Yet I will
Give my beloved
Kisses and kisses
Sweeter still.

3 Tell me, O, tell me,
Why should my kisses
Not be so?
For my old mother
Sweetened my kisses
Years ago.

Zpěvy Domova. Jan Seidl. (L. Mazáč, Prague, 1943.) As published in *Folk Songs of Europe* edited by Maude Karpeles. Copyright 1956 by Novello & Company.

136

The overlander
Australia

1. When I went out ex - plor - ing, I took up a fine new

run, And then came back to Syd- ney, and＿ had some jol - ly

fun; Then I want - ed stock for Queens- land, to ＿

Kemp sey I did wand - er, And bought a thou - sand

cat - tle there, and then turned __ o - ver - land - er.

Chorus:

So pass the bil - ly round boys, don't let the pint pot stand there,

For to - night we'll drink the health of ev - 'ry o - ver - land - er.

137 Good-bye, brother
BASIC U.S.A. (Spiritual)

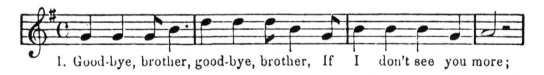

1. Good-bye, brother, good-bye, brother, If I don't see you more;

Now God bless you, now God bless you, If I don't see you more.

2 We part in de body but we meet in de spirit,
We'll meet in de heaben in de blessed • kingdom.

3 So good-bye, brother, good-bye, sister ;
Now God bless you, now God bless you.

* Glorious.

Reprinted by permission of Peter Smith from *Slave Songs of the United States* by William Allen, Charles Ware and Lucy Garrison. Original copyright 1897. Reprinted in 1951 by Peter Smith, New York.

138

BASIC

Fare ye well
U.S.A.

O fare you well, my brudder, fare you well by de

grace of God, For I'se gwin-en home; I'se gwin-en

home, my Lord, I'se gwinen home. Mas-sa Je-sus gib me a

lit-tle broom, For to sweep my heart clean;

Sweep 'em clean by de grace of God, An' glo-ry in my soul.

139

BASIC

No more rain fall for wet you
U.S.A. (Spiritual)

1. No more rain fall for wet you, Hal - le - lu, hal - le -

- lu, No more rain fall for wet you, Hal - le - lu - jah.

2 No more sun shine for burn you.

3 No more parting in de kingdom.

4 No more backbiting in de kingdom.

5 Every day shall be Sunday.

Reprinted by permission of Peter Smith from *Slave Songs of the United States* by William Allen, Charles Ware and Lucy Garrison. Original copyright 1897. Reprinted in 1951 by Peter Smith, New York.

140

BASIC

I want to go home
U.S.A. (Spiritual)

In chanting style.

1. Dere's no rain to | wet you. || O | yes, I want to go | home, || Want to go | home. ||

2 Dere's no sun to burn you.—O yes, etc.

3 Dere's no hard trials.

4 Dere's no whips a-crackin'.

5 Dere's no stormy weather.

6 Dere's no tribulation.

7 No more slavery in de kingdom.

8 No evil-doers in de kingdom.

9 All is gladness in de kingdom.

Reprinted by permission of Peter Smith from *Slave Songs of the United States* by William Allen, Charles Ware and Lucy Garrison. Original copyright 1897. Reprinted in 1951 by Peter Smith, New York.

141 Cocks are a-crowing
MODERATE *(Ils gials cumainzan a chantar)*
Switzerland

1. Ils gials cu-main - zan a chan - tar E la brü -
nett' a s'ap - pross - mar. Quel chi sto gua - dag -
nar seis pan, Nu dess dor - mir tar - da da - man.

1 Cocks are a-crowing at break of dawn
  And now begins another morn.
  And he who earns his daily bread,
  Must rise up early from his bed.

2 Rise up, rise up, good people all,
  Rise up, rise up, both great and small!
  Give thanks to God for your night's rest
  Go to your work with soul refreshed.

Liedermeie. Alfred Stern. (Hug, Zurich, 1952.) As published in *Folk Songs of Europe* edited by Maude Karpeles. Copyright 1956 by Novello & Company Limited.

142

BASIC

Crocodile song
Netherlands

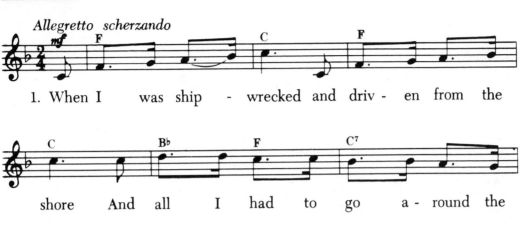

Allegretto scherzando

1. When I was ship - wrecked and driv - en from the

shore And all I had to go a - round the

coun - try to ex - plore, was my Right val - ar - i - ty,

whack val - ar - i - ty, chook val - ar - i - ty dey.

2. And steering up the other side I found the crocodile,
   From the tip of his nose to the end of his tail he was 10,000 miles,
   with a
      Right valarity, whack valarity, chook valarity dey.

3. The crocodile, you see, was not of the common race,
   For I had to get up a very tall pine for to look into his face,
      with a Right valarity, etc.

4. I bore away from his head one day with every stitch of sail,
   And going nine knots by the log in ten months reached his tail,
      with a Right valarity, etc.

5. The crocodile he set his mouth and thought he had his victim,
   But I went down his throat you see, and that is how I tricked him,
      with a Right valarity, etc.

143 On, roll on, my ball roll on
(En roulant ma boule roulant)
Canada
English: J. M. Gibbon

1. En rou-lant ma bou-le rou-lant, En rou-lant ma
1. On, roll on, my ball I roll on, On, roll on my

bou - le. Der - rièr' chez nous ya-t-un é - tang,
ball,___ on! 'Way back at home there is a pond,

En rou-lant ma bou-le, Trois beaux ca-nards s'en
On, roll on my ball, on! Three bon-nie ducks go

vont bai-gnant, Rou-li, rou-lant, ma bou-le rou-lant.
swim-ming'round, Roll on my ball, my ball I roll on.

From Folk Songs of the World. Copyright © 1966 by Charles Haywood. Reprinted by permission.

144 O now this glorious Eastertide
(Daar nu het feest van pasen is)
Netherlands

1 Daar nu .. het feest .. van Pa - sen is. Al -

le - lu - ja! Wij zin - gen van Heer Je - su Christ. Al -

Het levende Lied van Nederland. Jaap Kunst. (H.P. Paris, Amsterdam, 1947.) As published in *Folk Songs of Europe* edited by Maude Karpeles. Copyright 1956 by Novello & Company Limited.

le - lu - a ! A - le - lu - ja, .. Al - le - lu - ja !

1 O now this glorious Eastertide,

    Sing Hallelujah !

We'll sing of Christ who for us died.

    Sing Hallelujah,

    Sing Hallelujah, sing Hallelujah !

2 With joyful songs we'll praise His Name,

    For truly Christ is risen again.

3 And whether I go or whether I stay,

    My soul ever singing drives sorrow away.

145
BASIC

As I was going to Banbury
England

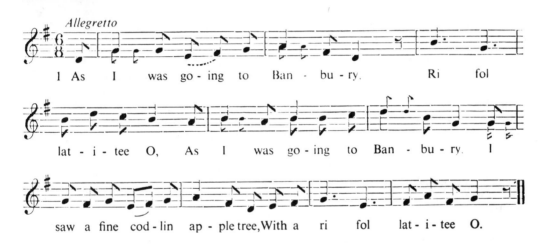

Allegretto

1 As I was go - ing to Ban - bu - ry.   Ri   fol

lat - i - tee O,   As   I   was go - ing to Ban - bu - ry.   I

saw a fine cod - lin ap - ple tree, With a   ri   fol   lat - i - tee O.

1 As I was going to Banbury,

    Ri fol lat-i-tee O,

As I was going to Banbury,

I saw a fine codlin apple tree,

    With a ri fol lat-i-tee O.

2 And when the codlins began to fall,

    I found five hundred men in all,

3 And one of the men I saw was dead,

    So I sent for a hatchet to open his head,

4 And in his head I found a spring,

    And seven young salmon a-learning to sing,

5 And one of the salmon as big as I,

    Now do you not think I am telling a lie?

6 And one of the salmon as big as an elf,

    If you want any more you must sing it yourself!

Folk-Songs (various). Cecil J. Sharp. (Novello, London, 1909.) As published in *Folk Songs of Europe* edited by Maude Karpeles.

146 Fivelgöer Christmas carol
MODERATE (Fivelgöer Kerstlied)
Netherlands

Andante

1 Wilt ach-ten waar-de huis-man schoon, Wat

ik U .. zal ver-ha-len, .. Hoe dat .. God zijn

ei-gen zoon Voor ons deed ne-der-da-len. ..

1 Come all you worthy gentlemen
And listen to my story,
How God did let His only Son
Descend from Heaven's glory.

2 He did from Heaven to earth come down,
His precious life He gave us.
Let all his chosen people sing:
O praise to Thee, Lord Jesus.

3 O he was born in Bethlehem
In an oxen stall so lowly ;
With wonder then did men behold
Lord Jesus Christ most Holy.

4 He is our blest Redeemer dear,
And we must not deny Him.
He will protect us to the end
And keep us ever nigh Him.

5 And now I wish to one and all,
To all good Christian gentlemen,
Good luck and all prosperity,
Now and for ever.   Amen.

Het levende Lied van Nederland. Jaap Kunst. (H.P. Paris, Amsterdam, 1947.) As published in *Folk Songs of Europe* edited by Maude Karpeles. Copyright 1956 by Novello & Company Limited.

147 Sea chantey
MODERATE (Shanadar)
England

Andante
SOLO   CHORUS

1 O Shan-a-dar, I love your daughter.   Hoo-ray, you rol-ling

SOLO   CHORUS

riv-er.   Shan-a-dar, I love your daugh-ter.   Ha

Capstan Chanteys. Cecil J. Sharp. (Novello, London, 1919.) As published in *Folk Songs of Europe* edited by Maude Karpeles.

ha, . . I'm bound a - way to the wild Mis - sou - ri.

1 O Shanadar, I love your daughter,
  Hooray, you rolling river.
  Shanadar, I love your daughter.
  Ha ha, I'm bound away to the wild Missouri.

2 O seven years I courted Sally.

3 And seven more I couldn't gain her.

4 She said I was a tarry sailor.

5 Farewell, my dear, I'm bound to leave you
  I'm bound away but will ne'er deceive you.

148
BASIC

Hark! the cock crows
(A'l chiante 'l gial)
Italy

Allegretto ma non troppo

1 A'l chian - te'l gial E cri - che'l dì, Man - di, ni -

ni - ne, . . . Man - di, ni - ni - ne, A'l chian - te'l gial

E cri - che'l dì, Man - di, ni - ni - ne, Me to - che par - tir.

1 Hark ! the cock crows,
  'Tis break of day.
  Good-bye, my darling,
  Good-bye, my darling.
  Hark ! the cock crows,
  'Tis break of day,
  Good-bye, my darling,
  For I must away.

2 Grieve not, my love,
  You have my heart.
  Good-bye, my darling,
  Good-bye, my darling.
  Grieve not, my love,
  You have my heart.
  Good-bye my darling,
  'Tis now we must part.

80 Canti della Montagna con Musica. Lion-Abanesi-Cornoldi. (Luciano Morpurgo, Roma, 1948.) As published in *Folk Songs of Europe* edited by Maude Karpeles. Copyright 1956 by Novello & Company Limited.

149

MODERATE

No other moon
(Luar do sertão)
Brazil
Trans.: G. Castiglione

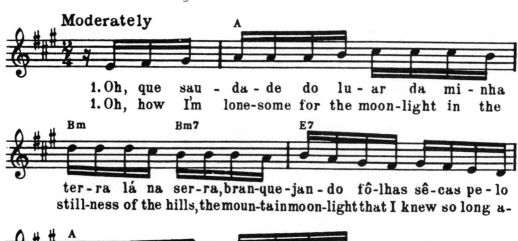

Moderately

1.Oh, que sau-da-de do lu-ar da mi-nha
1.Oh, how I'm lone-some for the moon-light in the

ter-ra lá na ser-ra, bran-que-jan-do fô-lhas sê-cas pe-lo
still-ness of the hills, the moun-tain moon-light that I knew so long a-

chão! Ês-te lu-ar, cá da ci-da-de, tão es-
go. The cit-y moon, so dark and lone-ly, leaves me

cu-ro, não tem a-que-la Sau-da-de do lu-ar lá do ser-tão.
cold and brings me on-ly lone-some yearn-ings for the moon I used to know

REFRAIN

Não há ó gen-te, oh, não lu-ar, co-mo ês-se do ser-
No oth-er moon on land or sea can be the same for

tão; Não há, o gen-te, oh, não lu-ar, co-mo ês-se do ser-tão.
me; No oth-er moon can ev-er be my moon of mem-o-ry.

Kiss ye the baby
(Cancão de Natal)
Portugal

Bei - jai o Me - ni - no, Bei - jai - o a -
go - ra; Bei - ja o Me - ni - no De Nos - sa Se - nho - ra. Bei -
jai o Me - ni - no De Nos - sa Se - nho - ra.
To - dos os pas - to - res Vão a Be - lém P'ra
ver o Me - ni - no Que a Se - nho - ra tem.

Come kiss ye the baby,
The newly born baby,
Come kiss ye the baby } (bis)
Of our Blessed Lady. }

    All the shepherds hasten
    To Bethany.
    The babe of Our Lady
    They have gone to see.

Noted by Artur Santos. As published in *Folk Songs of Europe* edited by Maude Karpeles. Copyright 1956 by Novello & Company Limited.

151 MODERATE

Boat-haulers' song
(A kak po lugu)
U.S.S.R.

1 In the fields the green, green grass
  Waves and glistens in the sun.
  Now the sun is sinking low
  And the day will soon be done.

2 And at dusk a young man comes,
  From his sorrows solace seeks,
  And his mother watches him,
  And to him she softly speaks:

3 Come, son, tell me whence your grief,
  Why do you thus hang your head?
  Why do you thus hang your head?
  'Tis as though all joys were dead.

Sbornik russkikh narodnykh pesen. M. Balakirev. (Belaieff, Leipzig, 1897.) As published in *Folk Songs of Europe* edited by Maude Karpeles. Copyright 1956 by Novello & Company Limited.

152 MODERATE

Groyle Machree
Canada

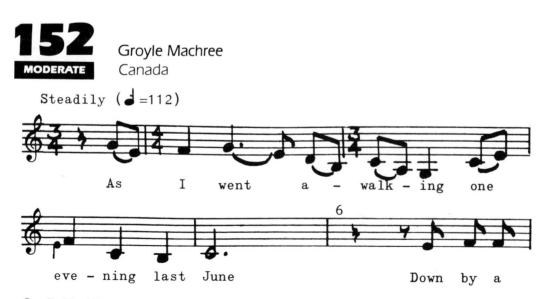

From *Traditional Singers and Songs from Ontario* edited by Edith Fowke. Copyright © 1965 by Folklore Associates, Inc. Reprinted by permission of Gale Research Co.

clear purl – ing ri – ver I

heard a sweet tune. It was

sung by a fair one whose voice was so

clear, Saying, "How hap – py would I

be if my true love were here."

VARIATIONS:

153 Twelve lads
MODERATE
(Fantje vasujejo)
Yugoslavia

1 Po pól pa fán - tou.. gré dwá - nàjst, Med ním je..
Já - nez.. tà trí - nàjst, Mój fànt se.. pa zmèd
u - sòh spoz - ná, Kan zé - len.. pú - šelc.. má.

O - dré - ja - ré - ja.. .dré - ja - róm, O - dré - ja -
- ré - ja.. .dré - ja - róm, O - dré - ja - ré - ja..
.dré - ja - róm, O - dré - ja - ré - ja - róm.

Across the fields twelve lads have gone,
With them as thirteenth goes my John,
All gay bedecked, he will not stay,
My love has gone away.

    My love has gone across the sea,
    My love, my dearest love leaves me,
    My love has gone across the sea,
    My dearest love leaves me.

Noted by France Marolt, 1930. As published in *Folk Songs of Europe* edited by Maude Karpeles. Copyright 1956 by Novello & Company Limited.

154 Shepherds, hark!
MODERATE
(Weihnachtslied)
Austria

1 Hört, ihre Hir - ten, und lasst euch sag'n, Was sich Neu's hat zu - ge - trag'n:

Burgenländische Volkslieder. Riedl-Klier. (Eisenstadt, 1950.) Noted by Karl M. Klier. As published in *Folk Songs of Europe* edited by Maude Karpeles. Copyright 1956 by Novello & Company Limited.

Ei - ne Jung - frau zart und rein Hat ge - bor'n ein Kin - de - lein,

Ei, . . ei, . . ei, ei, ei, In dem Stall auf ei - ner Streu.

1 Shepherds, hark! and listen well
To the tidings that I tell;
Of a Virgin pure and mild
Now is born a little child.
Be you glad, rejoice, this day!
On the straw where oxen lay.

2 All the choirs of Heaven raise
To this child their songs of praise
As with one accord they sing:
Glory to the heavenly King.
Be you glad, rejoice, this day!
Wondrous news the angels say.

3 They command us one and all
Now to go to Bethlem's stall,
There in swaddling clothes to find
Christ the Saviour of mankind
Be you glad, rejoice, this day!
In the manger on the hay.

4 Poor and weak this child we see,
But the Son of God is he;
Peace on earth he bringeth still
Unto men of right good will.
Be you glad, rejoice, this day!
Glory be to God alway!

Honey-ant song of Ljába
(Măkĕrénbĕn)
Australia
Trans.: T. G. H. Strehlow

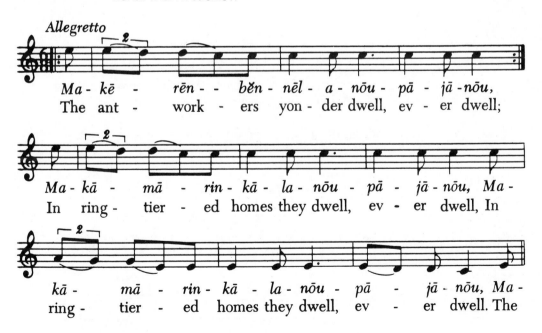

Allegretto

Ma - kē - - rēn - - bĕn nēl - a - nōu - pā - jā - nōu,
The ant - work - ers yon - der dwell, ev - er dwell;

Ma - kā - mā - rin - kā - la - nōu - pā - jā - nōu, Ma -
In ring - tier - ed homes they dwell, ev - er dwell, In

kā - mā - rin - kā - la - nōu - pā - jā - nōu, Ma -
ring - tier - ed homes they dwell, ev - er dwell. The

kē - rēn - bĕn - nēl - a nōu - pā - jā - nōu, Ma-
ant - work - ers yon - der dwell, ev - er dwell; The

kē - rēn - bĕn - nēl - a nōu - pā - jā - nōu. Ma-
ant - work - ers yon - der dwell, ev - er dwell; In

kā - mā - rin - kā - la - nōu - pā - jā - nou. Ma kā - mā - rin -
ring - tier - ed homes they dwell, ev - er dwell, In ring - tier - ed

kā - la - nōu - pā - jā - nōu. (Tones fade out—
homes they dwell, ev - er dwell. all notes are slurred)

156 Keel row

MODERATE New Zealand

Allegretto

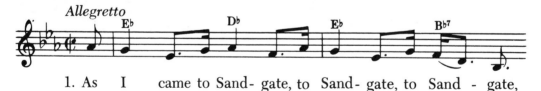

1. As I came to Sand- gate, to Sand- gate, to Sand- gate,

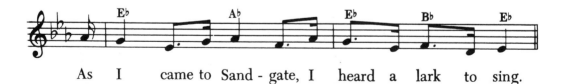

As I came to Sand - gate, I heard a lark to sing.

Chorus

Oh, well — may the keel row, the keel row, the keel — row,

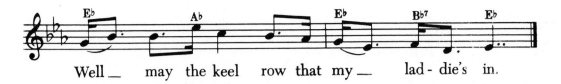

Well __ may the keel   row that my __ lad - die's in.

2. He wears a blue ribbon, blue ribbon, blue ribbon,
   He wears a blue ribbon, a dimple in his chin.

Chapter 13
Folk Songs in Minor Keys

OBSERVATIONS

Folk melodies in the minor mode are common to most countries. Texts may be sacred or secular, joyous or introspective. As in the previous chapter, chord suggestions are intended as a general guide for harmonization.

SUGGESTIONS

1. The problem scale degrees in minor are 1-2-3 and 6-7, using the tonic note as 1 (or "do" in movable do.) Intonation problems may be encountered: 3 is often too high; 6 and 7 are frequently too low, that is, they tend to be flat. Sing the melodic minor many times, *slowly*, with a well-tuned piano. Then vary the scale by inventing melodies such as:

$$1 \quad 3 \quad 2 \quad 5 \quad 7 \quad \text{(raised)}$$
$$5 \quad 1 \quad 6 \quad 7 \quad 1 \quad 3 \quad 1 \quad \text{etc.}$$

2. After the songs have been learned, try singing them as two-voice or three-voice canons; for example, 158 will produce "interesting" results as a two-voice canon at a time interval of four measures.

157 The birchbark song
BASIC (Nävervisan)
Sweden

Larghetto

1. E - ja mitt hjär ta, hur in - ner - lig är fröj - den.
Den lust och gläd je som un - nas mig av höj -

den. När jag be - tän - ker alt dö - dens län - ker Har

Chris - tus bru - tit och li - vet skän - ker Av nå - de.

Engel Lund. A Second Book of Folk-Songs. (Oxford University Press, London, 1947.) As published in Folk Songs of Europe edited by Maude Karpeles.

1 My heart, with inward peace, adores
                creation,
  Redeemed, my spirit goes to sure salvation.

For Christ lives now, his grace will show
That death is conquered, its pow'r brought
         low for ever.

2 Let me be ready, the hour of grace is nearing,
  To bring me home to see Christ's face
         appearing.

From sorrow, pain and grief set free,

From Heaven gather thy bride to thee
        for ever.

158

BASIC

Sigurd and Hamling
(Kong Diderik og Hans Kaemper)
Denmark

$\dot{} = 48$

1. De va - re vel syv .. og syv - sinds - ty - ve, Der de drog
ud fra Hald. Og der de kom - me til Brat - tings -
borg, .. Der slo - ge de de - res tjald. Det don - ner un - der
ros, de dan - ske hof - mænd der de ud - ri - de.

1 O seven and sev'nty warriors bold
  Rode out upon the plain,
  And when they came unto Brattingsborg
  They slackened their horse's rein.
    It thunders underfoot
    When proud Danish lords
    Go forth a-riding.

2 Then Sigurd he gave a mighty shout
  As he looked o'er the lea:
  O where's the man in all Denmark
  Will dare to fight with me?

Danmarks gamle Folkeviser (Copenhagen). Text: I (1853): melody: XI (1936). As published in *Folk Songs of Europe* edited by Maude Karpeles. Copyright 1956 by Novello & Company Limited.

The prisoner
(El Prisionero)
Spain

Moderato

1 Mes de Ma - yo, mes de Ma - yo, Cuan-do ha - ce la ca -
lor, Cuan - do los tri - gos en - ca - ñan Y es - tán
los camp - os en flor, Cuan - do los tri - gos en -
ca - ñan Y es - tán los camp - os en flor.

1 Month of Maying, month of Maying,
When the heat is on the land,
When the wheat in stalk is growing⎫
And in fields the flowers stand ; ⎭ *(bis)*

2 When the lark above is singing
To the nightingale her song
And the lovers out a-walking
Know the joy of love that's young.

3 But for me there's only waiting
In this prison like the grave ;
Sad am I, not even knowing
Whether night has turned to day.

4 Once a blackbird told the hour
As it sang to me at dawn,
But a bowman drew his arrow—
May God's curse be his reward.

El Folklore en la Escuela. Eduardo M. Torner. (Madrid, 1936.) As published in *Folk Songs of Europe* edited by Maude Karpeles. Copyright 1956 by Novello & Company Limited.

All on the grass
(Sur le gazon)
Belgium

Allegretto ma non troppo

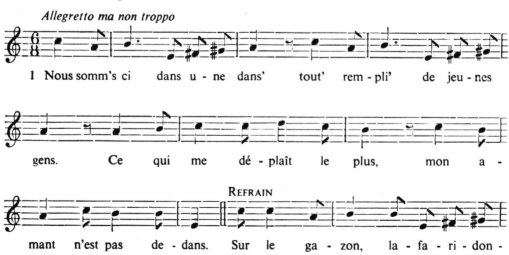

1 Nous somm's ci dans u - ne dans' tout' rem - pli' de jeu - nes
gens. Ce qui me dé - plaît le plus, mon a -

REFRAIN

mant n'est pas de - dans. Sur le ga - zon, la - fa - ri - don -

Wallonie, IX. (1901.) Noted by Oscar Colson at Liège. As published in *Folk Songs of Europe* edited by Maude Karpeles. Copyright 1956 by Novello & Company Limited.

daine, Ve - nez, mou - tons, la - fa - ri - don - don.

1 Here we dance all hand in hand, men and
   maids on the green grass.
 I am sad because my love in the dance
   cannot be found.
   All on the grass, a roodle dum day,
   Come, lambkin, dance, a roodle dum
   dee.

2 I am sad because my love in the dance
   cannot be found.
   But I see him from afar riding on a piebald
   horse.

161 MODERATE Down the street
(Vdol Pa Ulitzye)
U.S.S.R.
Trans.: H. Haufrecht and S. Jurist

Somewhat slowly and freely

1. Vdol pa u - li - tzye me - te - li - tza me tyot,
1. Down the street a blind - ing snow-storm ra - ges strong,

Za ___ me - te - li - tzei moy mi - len - koy i - dyot. ___
In ___ the midst of it my dear one walks a - long. ___

"Ty pa - stoy, pa - stoy, ___ kra - sa - vi - tza ma - ya, -
"Wait a - while, just wait, ___ my dar - ling so fair

Da - zvol na - gle - det - sia, ra - dost na te - bia!" ___ bia!"
Let me but ad - mire you, 'Pon you let me stare." stare!"

2. **Let me gaze upon your beauty and your grace,**
   Let me look upon your fair and gentle face. **REFRAIN**

3. **Since I first saw you I've simply lost my mind.**
   You are my only cure, so won't you please be kind. **REFRAIN**

162

MODERATE

Negev desert dance
(Hora Hanegev)
Israel
Trans.: H. Haufrecht and D. Gerlich

Lively

Ze - mer ze - mer lach, ze - mer ze - mer lach,
We shall sing a song, We shall sing a song,

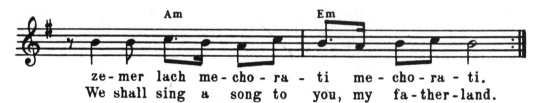

ze - mer lach me - cho - ra - ti me - cho - ra - ti.
We shall sing a song to you, my fa - ther - land.

Ha - ra - ra - ich he - ma yis - ma - chu
Then will glad - ness cov - er your moun - tains

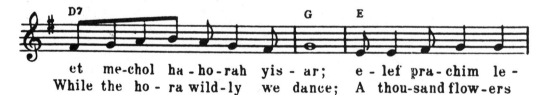

et me - chol ha - ho - rah yis - ar; e - lef pra - chim le -
While the ho - ra wild - ly we dance; A thou - sand flow - ers

fe - ta yif - ra - chu vi - chu - su et pne ha - mid - bar.
will bloom from foun - tains cov - er - ing the dry des - ert sands

For a kiss
(Por un beso)
Columbia
Trans.: H. Yurchenco
and H. Haufrecht

The Vito
(El vito)
Spain
Trans.: P. Kresh

2. All of gold are girls unmated,
   All of silver, those that married,
   All the widows, copper-plated,
   All of tin, the old who tarried.   **REFRAIN**

165

MODERATE

O, Ola, Ola
(Aa Ola, Ola, min eigen onge!)
Norway

Slowly

1. Aa O - la, O - la, min ei - en
1. Oh O - la, O - la, my own be -

On - ge! kvi la' du paa meg den Sorg saa
lov - ed, Why have you left me with sor - rows

ton - ge? Eg taenk - te al - dri du brydd' deg
cov - ered? I nev - er thought you would be un -

om, aa nar - re meg, som du saag va'
true, Since I was young as you full - well

ong, aa nar - re meg, som du saag va' ong. __
knew, Since I was young as you full - well knew. __

2. Oh, many tears down my cheeks were flowing,
I often thought that my mind was going,
And I have cried just as many tears
As there are days in a thousand years,
As there are days in a thousand years.

Chapter 14
Folk Songs Using Modal Resources

OBSERVATIONS

As previously indicated, *modal* is the term used to classify melodies in this chapter that contain a lowered leading tone and therefore includes songs in *Aeolian* mode (natural minor). Precise rhythm and perfect intonation remain primary goals.

SUGGESTIONS

1. Identify the mode of each folk song, using the following general guide:

   Dorian is the same as natural minor with a raised sixth degree of scale.

   Phrygian is as natural minor with a lowered second scale degree.

   Lydian is the same as a major scale with a raised fourth scale degree.

   Mixolydian is the same as major with a lowered seventh scale degree.

   (Aeolian and natural minor are identical.)
2. Practice singing these modes, emphasizing variants from the better known major and natural minor formations.

166
BASIC

The two maidens
(Två Jungfrur)
Finland

Andante

1 Det gin - go två jung - frur i ro - sen - de - lund, De
plo - cka - de blom-mor och bla - der. Den e - na hon var så
hjär - te - ligt glad, Den and - ra var så sorg-sen och be - drö - vad.

1 Two maids in a garden were walking one day
A-picking the lilies and roses,
And one of the maidens was happy and gay,
The other so sadly was sighing.

2 The rich maiden thus to the poor one did say:
O what is the cause of your sorrow?
My sorrow is all for the comely young lad
That both you and I love so dearly.

Du Sköna Sang. Ragnar Hollmérus & Otto Andersson. (Forlaget Bro, Åbo, 1946.) As published in *Folk Songs of Europe* edited by Maude Karpeles. Copyright 1956 by Novello & Company Limited.

3 The young man was standing not far from
>that place
And heard what the maidens were saying.
He cast up his eyes to the heavens above
And asked which of them he should marry.

4 O if I should marry the maid that is rich,
And take not the one that is poorer,
O then she will weep and will grieve all her
>days;
I fear that her heart will be broken.

5 And if I should marry the maid that is **poor**
And take not the one that is richer,
O then she will find her another young man
And with him she'll live and be happy.

6 The young man stepped forward in front
>of them both,
And gave his right hand to the poor one.
Now I am your lover and you shall be mine;
For ever we'll live with each other.

Little partridge
(Perdikitza)
Greece

1 Little partridge, our greetings we are
>bringing,

Songs of joy on this bridal morn we're
>singing.

2 Like a bird in her nest your young ones
>bearing,

May you tenderly for their needs be caring.

3 Though your nest be by wind and tempest
>shaken,

Yet your young ones must never be for-
>saken.

4 May your children be like the summer
>flowers

Shedding fragrance amongst the shady
>bowers.

Greek Folk Songs. George Pachtikos. (Athens, 1905.) As published in *Folk Songs of Europe* edited by Maude Karpeles. Copyright 1956 by Novello & Company Limited.

168
BASIC

Lullaby
(Fi la nana)
Italy

F la na - na, e mi bel fiol, Fi la

na - na, e mi bel fiol, Fa si la na - na.

Dor - mi ben, e mi bel fiol, Dor - mi ben, e mi bel

fiol, Fa si la na - na.

Hush-a-bye, my little babe, (*bis*)
And sleep till daybreak.
Sweetly sleep, my little babe, (*bis*)
O sleep till daybreak.

Trenta Ninne Nanne Popolare Italiane. Giusepppe Mulè. (Alberto de Santis, Roma, 1934.) As published in *Folk Songs of Europe* edited by Maude Karpeles. Copyright 1956 by Novello & Company Limited.

169 The maid of Newfoundland

MODERATE *Newfoundland*

Lento con rubato

1. Ye __ mu - ses mine, with me com - bine; Your aid __ I __ do in -

vite To sing in praise __ of her I love, My __

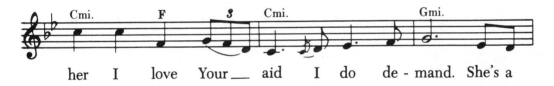

own sweet - heart's de - light; To sing in praise __ of

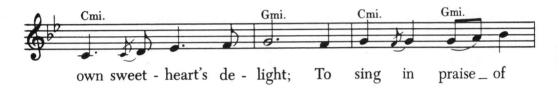

her I love Your __ aid I do de - mand. She's a

maid - en fair, I do de - clare, And __ she dwells in New - found - land.

2.

The diamond sparkles bright and clear
In many a queenly crown;
The virgin pearl beneath the sea
Lies many a fathom down;
The diamond, pearl, and peerless gem
Of Africa's sunny strand
Cannot compare, I do declare,
With the maid of Newfoundland.

3.

I've seen the maids of many lands
On many a foreign shore,
The French, the Greek, the Portuguese,
Likewise the swarthy Moor,
Chinese, Malay, and Austrian maids,
And the girls of Hindustan,—
But for beauty rare, they can't compare
With the maid of Newfoundland.

From Folk Songs of the World. Copyright © 1966 by Charles Haywood. Reprinted by permission.

Peter Gray
U.S.A.

From *Our Singing Country* collected, adapted and arranged by John A. Lomax and Alan Lomax. TRO—© Copyright 1941 and renewed 1969 by Ludlow Music, Inc., New York, N.Y. Used by permission.

Katie Kádár
(Kádár Kata)
Transylvania

Magyar Népzene. Zoltán Kodály. (Universal Edition, London, 1929.) As published in *Folk Songs of Europe* edited by Maude Karpeles. Copyright 1956 by Novello & Company Limited.

1 I'm in love with Katie Kádár.
  May we marry, O dear mother?
  Though the daughter of a bondsman,
  Dearly we do love each other.

2 Son, you shall not wed beneath you ;
  You shan't marry Kádár's daughter.
  In the lake I'd rather drown her,
  Throw her body in deep water.

3 Go fetch me my chestnut pony;
  Here no longer will I tarry,
  I'll go forth to some far country,
  Since my true love I can't marry.

4 He went riding to far countries,
  Ever on his sweetheart pond'ring,
  Till he met a fellow-trav'ller
  In a lonely forest wand'ring.

Ploughing song
(Petit laboureur)
France

1 O ploughman O ho!
  Your furrows are not straight.
  Did you not say, my master,
  Your oxen I should take? O lay.
    Pull up, O pull, lay O, O ho,
    Lay ay O ho lay ay.

2 No, ploughman, no, no,
  You have not heard me right.
  Did you not say, my master,
  One hundred francs were mine? O lay

Collected and noted by Cl. Marcel-Dubois and M. Andral. As published in *Folk Songs of Europe* edited by Maude Karpeles. Copyright 1956 by Novello & Company Limited.

173

MODERATE

Lord Gregory
Scotland

Very free

"Oh, moth-er, I had a warn-ing dream, Oh,

moth - er, I had a dream. I

dreamed the bon-ny lass of Loch-land Lane, She was

tap - ping to get in."

VARIATIONS:

2. "Lie down, lie down, Lord Gregory,
   Lie down and take a sleep.
   It was just an hour and a half ago
   She was tapping at your gate."

3. "Oh, you vile woman! Oh, you vile woman!
   Oh, you vile woman, you!
   Why didn't you rise and let her in
   Or even waken me?"

4. "Oh, sell to me your gray mare,
   Or sell to me the brown,
   Or sell to me the fastest horse
   That ever a man rode on."

The cuckoo
England

2 As I was a-walking and a-talking one day,
I met my own true love, as he came that way,
O to meet him was a pleasure, though the courting was a woe,
For I found him false-hearted, he would kiss me and go.

3 I wish I were a scholar and could handle the pen,
I would write to my lover and to all roving men.
I would tell them of the grief and woe that attend on their lies,
I would wish them have pity on the flower when it dies.

English Folk Songs (Selected Edition), I. Cecil J. Sharp. (Novello, London, 1920.) As published in *Folk Songs of Europe* edited by Maude Karpeles.
Copyright 1922 by Novello & Company Limited. Copyright renewed 1950.

175

MODERATE

Maiden of the dark brown hair
(Nighean dubh's a nighean donn)
Scotland

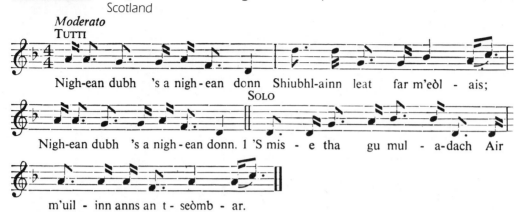

Moderato
TUTTI

Nigh-ean dubh 's a nigh-ean donn Shiubhl-ainn leat far m'eòl - ais;

SOLO

Nigh-ean dubh 's a nigh-ean donn. 1 'S mis - e tha gu mul - a-dach Air

m'uil - inn anns an t - seòmb - ar.

Maiden of the dark brown hair,
Far with her I'd wander,
Maiden of the dark brown hair.

1 Long have I been waiting here
Alone and full of sorrow.

2 I outside behind the house
While you inside are courting.

3 East and west I'd walk with you
Without my horse and bridle.

4 Through the Sound of Mull I'd go,
Nor wait to put my shoes on.

5 To Kintyre I'd go with you,
Where I was well acquainted.

6 I would go to Uist with you
Where barley ripens golden.

7 I would reach the stars with you,
If your own folk were willing.

8 I would reach the moon with you,
If you would say we'll marry.

Folksongs and Folklore of South Uist. Margaret Fay Shaw. (Routledge & Kegan Paul, London, 1955.) As published in *Folk Songs of Europe* edited by Maude Karpeles. Copyright 1956 by Novello & Company Limited.

176

MODERATE

Ay la le lo
Spain

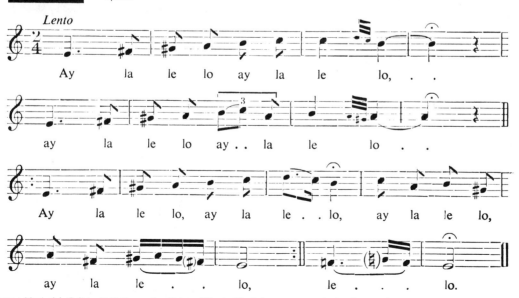

Lento

Ay la le lo ay la le lo, . .

ay la le lo ay .. la le lo .

Ay la le lo, ay la le .. lo, ay la le lo,

ay la le . . lo, le . . lo.

Cancionero Musical de Galicia, II. C. Sampedo y Folgar. (Diputación de las cuatro provincias, Pontevedra, 1942.) As published in *Folk Songs of Europe* edited by Maude Karpeles.

Dance of zalongo
(Khoros tou zalongou)
Greece

1 Farewell, farewell, land of sorrow (*bis*).
   Farewell, this sweet life we leave. (*bis*)
       Farewell, ye little fountains,
       Ye valleys, streams and mountains. } (*bis*)

2 Suli women will not live in slav'ry;
   Rather they would welcome death.

3 As if to the fair they walk proudly
   Lilac in full blossom they bear.

4 O down they go unto Hades
   With dance and with songs of joy.

Neohellenic Folk Music. Solon Michaelides. (Limassol, Cyprus, 1948.) As published in *Folk Songs of Europe* edited by Maude Karpeles. Copyright 1956 by Novello & Company Limited.

Chapter 15
Folk Songs Employing Mixed Modes

OBSERVATIONS

Chapter 15 provides some of the most interesting melodies of the entire text. The chapter includes pentatonic (five-note) scales; melodies ending on a scale degree other than 1, 3, or 5; melodies with two different forms of the third scale degree; or simply non-classified scales such as 189: e f g# a b d (e). This great literature comes, after all, from oral traditions and the diversity is at once its charm and its strength.

SUGGESTIONS

1. After singing the folk song, write out the pitches of the melody in scalar form. Sing these "synthetic" scales several times then sing the melody again—this time more rapidly and with perfect intonation.
2. Rhythmic exercises involving odd meters should be devised. Please see Examples 189 and 190 in "Bulgarian rhythm."

178 Arirang

MODERATE   Korea

With a lilt

A - ri - rang,   A - ri - rang,   A - ra - ri - o,
A - ri - rang,   A - ri - rang,   A - ra - ri - o,

A - ri - rang,   ko - gay - ro   nau - mau - kan - da.
Like the stars, my   tears are count-less as they cease-less-ly   flow!

opt.

Nah - rul   pau - ri - go,   kah si   noon nim - eun
You,   so   faith-less are   leav - ing   me a - lone and pale;

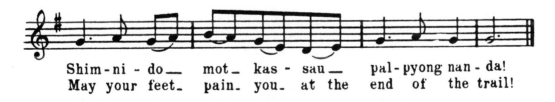

Shim - ni - do   mot   kas - sau   pal - pyong nan - da!
May your feet   pain   you   at the   end of   the trail!

From *Korea, Land of Song* published by the Korean Research and Information Office. We have been unable to contact the copyright holder. Any information as to their whereabouts would be appreciated.

179 Hallelu, hallelu

MODERATE
U.S.A. (spiritual)

1. Oh one day as an - od - er, Hal - le - lu, hal - le -

lu! 2. When de ship is out a - sail - in', Hal - le - lu - jah!

3 Member walk and never tire.

4 Member walk Jordan long road.

5 Member walk tribulation.

6 You go home to Wappoo.

7 Member seek new repentance.

8 I go to seek my fortune.

9 I go to seek my dying Saviour.

10 You want to die like Jesus.

Reprinted by permission of Peter Smith from *Slave Songs of the United States* by William Allen, Charles Ware and Lucy Garrison. Original copyright 1897. Reprinted in 1951 by Peter Smith, New York.

180 Children do linger

MODERATE
U.S.A. (spiritual)

1. O member, will you lin - ger? See de chil - 'en do

lin - ger here. 2. I go to glo - ry wid you, Member, join.

3 O Jesus is our Captain.

Reprinted by permission of Peter Smith from *Slave Songs of the United States* by William Allen, Charles Ware and Lucy Garrison. Original copyright 1897. Reprinted in 1951 by Peter Smith, New York.

Down the mountain
(Tečie potok od Kriváňa mútny)
Czechoslovakia

1 Down the mountain angry waters leaping,
What has brought you, love, so near to
weeping?
Do the waters pour their pain upon you?
Or perhaps the friends who fawn upon you?

2 Angry waters pour no pain upon me,
And my friends I never see; they shun me.
Ten long weeks have heavy eyelids burned
me,
Ten long weeks have sleep and friends both
spurned me.

3 I was false. Another I went wooing.
False to love, I was my own undoing.
To her death my love went in this torrent,
Left her sorrows here—and left me torment.

12 *Ľudových pieśni slovenských*. Zdeněk Folprecht. (Hudební Matice umelěcké besedy, Prague, 1940.) As published in *Folk Songs of Europe* edited by Maude Karpeles. Copyright 1956 by Novello & Company Limited.

182

MODERATE

The exile
(Pa mëmë)
Albania

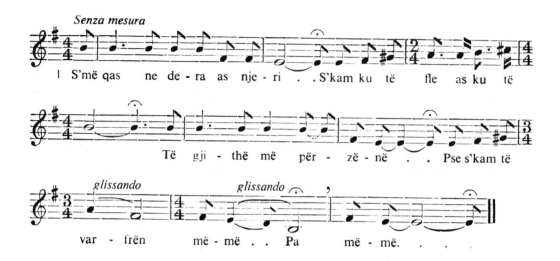

I S'më qas   ne de - ra as nje - ri . .S'kam ku të   fle   as ku të

Të gji - thë më për - zë - në . . Pse s'kam të

var - frën   më - më . . Pa   më - më. . .

1 O I have neither hearth nor home,
   From door to door all day I roam,
   And bitterly I suffer
   Without my dearest mother.
         O, mother.

2 And all around me I can see
   The children playing happily.
   They're laughing with each other
   Whilst I am weeping, mother.
         O, mother.

3 For here, unhappy and alone,
   I am a wand'rer far from home.
   O where are you, my mother ?
   My heart is breaking, mother.
         O, mother.

Noted by Patrick Shuldham-Shaw from Sami Butko, London, 1954. As published in *Folk Songs of Europe* edited by Maude Karpeles. Copyright 1956 by Novello & Company Limited.

183

MODERATE

In the garden a beggar there was
(Nan da vanathil or andi)

India
English: L. Natarajan
and H. Haufrecht

Moderately slow

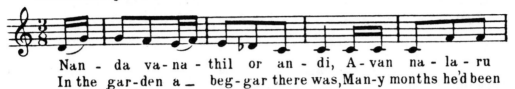

Nan - da va - na - thil or an - di, A - van na - la - ru
In the gar-den a _ beg-gar there was, Man-y months he'd been

ma - da - mai, Ku - ya - va - nai ven - di. _ Kon -
beg-ging the pot-ter for a clay _ vase. _ Once he

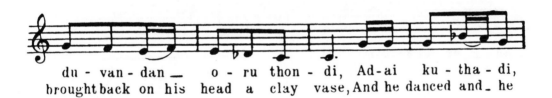

du - van - dan _ o - ru thon - di, Ad - ai ku - tha - di,
brought back on his head a clay vase, And he danced and _ he

3

ku - tha - di, Po - tu - dai - chan - di! _
danced till _ the vase _ fell and went _ smash! _

_ Nan - da va - na - thil or an - di.
_ In the gar - den a _ beg - gar there was.

Zum gali, gali
Israel

Moderately

Chorus:
Zum ga-li, ga-li, ga-li, Zum, ga-li, ga-li,

Solo: He-cha-lutz le' - man a-vo-dah,___
Chorus:
Zum ga-li, ga-li, ga-li, zum ga-li, ga-li, Zum (etc.) A-vo-dah le'
Solo:

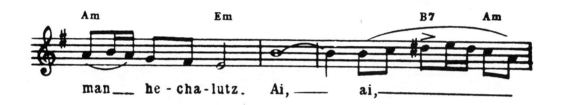

man___ he-cha-lutz. Ai,___ ai,___

Ai,___ ai,___ Ai,___ hai___ hai-ah, hai-ah,

Chorus and Solo:
Zum ga-li ga-li, ga-li, Zum ga-li, ga-li, Zum.

Zum gali, gali, gali, etc.
The pioneer does the work,
Zum gali, gali, gali, etc.
The work is done by the pioneer.

Ay, ay, ay, ay,
Ay, life, life, life,
Zum gali, gali, gali, etc.

185

MODERATE

The keys of the jail
(Les clefs de la prison)
American

Fast ♩=88

THE BOY

Chère mom! _____ On vient m'don-ner les ___ clefs, ___ Les

clefs de la ___ pri - son, Les clefs de la pri - son. _____

HIS MOTHER

Gar' - tu! Com-ment dis - tu _____ te ___ donne ___ Les clefs de

la pri - son, ___ En quant les of - fi - ciers ___ Les a cro - chées dans l'cou, ___

___ Les a cro - chées dans _____ l'cou. _____

THE BOY: Dear Mom! They just gave me the keys of the jail, the keys of the jail.

HIS MOTHER: Look here! How can you say gave you the keys of the jail, when the policemen have hooked them in your neck, hooked them in your neck.

186 John Henry

U.S.A.

1 Well, every Monday mornin'
   When the bluebirds begin to sing,
   You can hear those hammers a mile or mo',
   You can hear John Henry's hammer ring, oh, Lawdy,
   Hear John Henry's hammer ring.

2 John Henry told his old lady,
   "Will you fix my supper soon?
   Got ninety miles o' track I've got to line,
   Got to line it by the light of the moon, oh, Lawdy,
   Line it by the light o' the moon."

3 John Henry had a little baby,
   He could hold him out in his hand;
   But the last word I heard that po' child say,
   "My dad is a steel-drivin' man, oh, Lawdy,
   Daddy is a steel-drivin' man."

187

ADVANCED

Fare ye well, my darlin'
U.S.A.

Moderately slow ♩=88

So fare ye well, my darl - in', so fare ye well, my dear,

Don't__ grieve for my long ab - sence, while I am pres - ent here.

Since it is__ my mis - for - tune a sol - dier for to be,

Oh, try to live con - tent - ed and do__ not grieve for me.

1 So fare ye well, my darlin', so fare ye well, my dear,
Don't grieve for my long absence, while I am present here.
Since it is my misfortune a soldier for to be,
Oh, try to live contented and do not grieve for me.

2 She wrung her lily-white hands and so mournful she did cry,
"You've enlisted as a soldier and in the war you'll die.
In the battle you'll be wounded and in the center be slain;
It'll burst my heart asunder if I'll never see you again."

188 O dance, you maids
MODERATE
(Pkiaste kopelles, sto choro)
Cyprus

1 O dance, you maids, be blithe and gay (*bis*)

When you are young, 'tis time to play,

O dance, you maids be blithe and gay.

2 O dance, while you have time to spend (*bis*)

Before you have a babe to tend. (*bis*)

3 Before your toil it does begin (*bis*)

O that's the time to dance and sing (*bis*)

4 When you your single life do quit (*bis*)

Then in your corner you must sit. (*bis*)

Cyprus Folk Music. Th. Kallinicos. (Nicosia, 1951.) As published in *Folk Songs of Europe* edited by Maude Karpeles. Copyright 1956 by Novello & Company Limited.

189 Rugged mountain slopes
ADVANCED
(Blazhena stara-planina)
Bulgaria

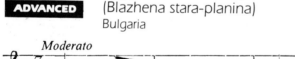

1 Well belov'd, rugged mountain slopes,

Well belov'd, rugged mountain slopes,

2 Fill'd at all seasons of the year.

Winter days bring the shepherds here.

3 Outlaw bands come in summer days.

Each bush hides one brave outlawed man.

4 Each tree hides one brave outlaw's gun,

Each rock hides banners of the brave.

Das Bulgarische Volkslied. Christo Obreschkoff. (Kurth, Paul Haupt, Bern and Leipzig.) Noted by R. Katzarova. As published in *Folk Songs of Europe* edited by Maude Karpeles. Copyright 1956 by Novello & Company Limited.

A brave companion
(Ogŭn gori na balkana)
Bulgaria

1 Огъ - ън го - ри на бал - ка - на Виж - дам го

гле - дам го, Дай ми, ма - мо вя - рен дру - гар

|1. Да ид - а, да ви - дя |2. Да ида, . . да ви дя.

1 Fires are burning in the mountain.⎫ (bis)
  Mother, I'd fain go too.   ⎭
  Let me seek a brave companion,⎫ (bis)
  Mother, I beg of you.   ⎭

2 Daughter, daughter, seek your brother.
  He'll guide you on your way.
  Whether false or whether trusty
  By him I would not stay.

3 Well, my daughter, seek your father.
  He'll guide you on your way.
  Whether false or whether trusty,
  By him I would not stay.

4 Then, my daughter, find your true love.
  With him you'll surely stay.
  Yes, he's true and brave and trusty,
  He'll guide me on my way.

Narodni Pesni ot Sredna Severna Bulgaria. Vassil Stoin. (Izdava Ministerstvoto Na Narodnoto Prosveshchenie, Sofia, 1931.) As published in *Folk Songs of Europe* edited by Maude Karpeles. Copyright 1956 by Novello & Company Limited.

FURTHER SUGGESTED STUDIES

Most music libraries will have a considerable collection of folk songs. These volumes can provide an abundance of sight-reading material for the singer and instrumentalist alike. For keyboard players, the ability to accompany folk songs at sight (by improvisation of appropriate harmonies) is a standard component of musicianship.

For elementary theoretical studies in harmony, folk materials provide an excellent basis for the investigation of logical and natural progression and harmonic order. Materials of Chapters 12–15 can be a rewarding supplement to "keyboard harmony" exercises.

Appendix

Latin Pronunciation Guide

The following tables indicate approximately the sounds of Latin and how the letters were used by the Romans to represent those sounds.

VOWELS

LONG	SHORT
ā as in *father*: **dās, cārā**	ă as in *Dinah*: **dăt, căsă**
ē as in *they*: **mē, sēdēs**	ĕ as in *pet*: **ĕt, sĕd**
ī as in *machine*: **hīc, sīcā**	ĭ as in *pin*: **hĭc, sĭccă**
ō as in *clover*: **ōs, mōrēs**	ŏ as in *orb, off*: **ŏs, mŏră**
ū as in *rude*: **tū, sūmō**	ŭ as in *put*: **tŭm, sŭm**

y as in French *tu* or German *über*

DIPHTHONGS

ae as *ai* in *aisle*: **cārae, saepe**

au as *ou* in *house*: **aut, laudō**

ei as in *reign*: **deinde**

eu as Latin **e + u**, pronounced rapidly as a single syllable: **seu**. The sound is not found in English and is rare in Latin.

oe as *oi* in *oil*: **coepit, proelium**

ui as in Latin **u + i**, spoken as a single syllable. This diphthong occurs only in **huius, cuius, huic, cui, hui**. Elsewhere the two letters are spoken separately as in **fu‑it, frūctu‑ī**.

CONSONANTS

Latin consonants had the same sounds as the English consonants with the following exceptions:

bs and **bt** were pronounced *ps* and *pt* (e.g., **urbs, obtineō**); otherwise Latin **b** had the same sound as our letter (e.g., **bibēbant**).

c was always hard as in *can*, never soft as in *city*: **cum, civis, facilis**.

g was always hard as in *get*, never soft as in *gem*: **glōria, gerō**.

i was usually a consonant with the sound of *y* as in *yes* when used before a vowel at the beginning of a word (**iūstus** = yustus); between two vowels within a word it served in double capacity: as the vowel *i* forming a diphthong with the preceding vowel, and as the consonant *y* (**reiectus** = rei‑yectus, **maior** = mai‑yor, **cuius** = cui‑yus): otherwise it was usually a vowel.

r was trilled: **cūrāre, retrahere**.

s was always voiceless as in *see*; never voiced as in our word *ease*: **sed, posuissēs, mīsistis**.

t always had the sound of *t* as in *tired*, never of *sh* as in *nation*: **taciturnitās, nātiōnem, mentiōnem**.

v had the sound of our *w*: **vīvō** = wīwō, **vīnum** = wīnum.

x had the sound of *ks* as in *axle*; not of *gz* as in *exert*: **mixtum, exerceō**.

ch represented Greek *chi* and had the sound of *ckh* in *block head*, not of *ch* in *church*: **chorus, Archilochus**.

ph represented Greek *phi* and had the sound of *ph* in *up hill*, not of *ph* in our pronunciation of *philosophy*: **philosophia**.

th represented Greek *theta* and had the sound of *th* in *hot house*, not of *th* in *thin* or *the*: **theātrum**.

The Romans quite appropriately pronounced double consonants as two separate consonants; we in our haste or slovenliness usually render them as a single consonant. For instance, the **rr** in the Latin word **currant** sounded like the two *r*'s in *the cur ran*; and the **tt** in **admittent** sounded like the two *t*'s in *admit ten*.

SYLLABLES

A Latin word has as many syllables as it has vowels or diphthongs.

In dividing a word into syllables:

From pp. xxxi–xxxiii in LATIN: AN INTRODUCTORY COURSE BASED ON ANCIENT AUTHORS, Third Edition by Frederic M. Wheelock (Barnes & Noble, Inc.). Copyright © 1963 by Harper & Row, Publishers, Inc. Reprinted by permission of the publisher.

1. Two contiguous vowels or a vowel and a diphthong are separated: **dea, de–a; deae, de–ae.**

2. A single consonant between two vowels goes with the second vowel: **amīcus, a–mī–cus.**

3. When two or more consonants stand between two vowels, the last consonant goes with the second vowel: **mittō, mit–tō; servāre, ser–vā–re; cōn-sūmptus, cōn–sūmp–tus.** However, a stop (**p, b, t, d, c, g**) + a liquid (**l, r**) count as a single consonant and go with the following vowel: **patrem, pa–trem; castra, cas–tra.** Also counted as single consonants are **ch, ph, th,** and **qu: architectus, ar–chi–tec–tus; loquācem, lo–quā–cem.**

A syllable is long *by nature* if it has a long vowel or a diphthong; a syllable is long *by position* if it has a short vowel followed by two or more consonants or **x,** which is a double consonant (=*ks*). Otherwise a syllable is short.

Syllables long by nature: *lau–dō, cā–rae, a–mī–cus.*

Syllables long by position: **lau–*dan*–tem, mī-*sis*–se, *ax*–is** (=*ak–sis*).

ACCENT

In a word of two syllables the accent falls on the first syllable: **sér–vo, sa'e–pe, ní–hil.**

In a word of three or more syllables (1) the accent falls on the syllable which is *second* from the end if that syllable is long (**ser–vá–re, cōn–sér–vat, for-tú–na**); (2) otherwise, the accent falls on the syllable which is *third* from the end (**mó–ne–ō, pá–tri–a, pe–cú–ni–a, vó–iu–cris**).

French Pronunciation Guide

FRENCH LETTER	DESCRIPTION OF PRONUNCIATION
a, à	Between *a* in *calm* and *a* in *hat.*
â	Like *a* in *calm.*
ai	Like *e* in *bed.*
au	Like *oa* in *coat.*
b	As in English. At end of words, usually silent.
c	Before *e, i, y,* like *s.* Elsewhere, like *k.* When *c* occurs at the end of a word and is preceded by a consonant, it is usually silent.
ç	Like *s.*
cc	Before *e, i,* like *x.* Elsewhere, like *k.*
ch	Usually like *sh* in *short.* *ch* is pronounced like *k* in words of Greek origin; before *a, o,* and *u; and before consonants.*
d	At beginning and in middle of words, as in English. At end of words, usually silent.
e	At end of words, normally silent; indicates that preceding consonant letter is pronounced. Between two single consonant sounds, usually silent. Elsewhere, like English *a* in *sofa.*
é	Approximately like *a* in *hate.*
è, ê, ei	Like *e* in *bed.*
eau	Like *au.*
ent	Silent when it is the third person plural ending.
er (End of Words)	At end of words of more than one syllable, usually like *a* in *hate,* the *r* being silent; otherwise like *air* in *chair.*
es	Silent at end of words.
eu	A vowel sound not found in English; like French *e,* but pronounced with the lips rounded as for *o.*
ez	At end of words almost always like English *a* in *hate,* the *z* being silent.
f	As in English; silent at the end of a few words.
g	Before *e, i, y,* like *z* in *azure.* Elsewhere, like *g* in *get.* At end of words, usually silent.
gn	Like *ni* in *onion.*
gu	Before *e, i, y;* like *g* in *get.* Elsewhere, like *g* in *get* plus French *u* (see below).

Concise Pronunciation Guides to French, German, and Italian reproduced by permission from THE RANDOM HOUSE DICTIONARY, *Unabridged Edition,* pp. 1697, 1791, 1836. Copyright © 1954, 1957, 1959 by Random House, Inc.

h   In some words, represents a slight tightening of the throat muscles (in French, called "aspiration").

In most words, silent.

i, i   Like *i* in *machine*.

ill   (-il at end of words) like *y* in *yes*, in many but not all words.

j   Like *z* in *azure*.

k   As in English.

l   As in English, but always pronounced "bright," with tongue in front of mouth.

m, n   When double, and when single between two vowel letters or at beginning of word, like English *m* and *n* respectively.

When single at end of syllable (at end of word or before another consonant), indicates nasalization of preceding vowel.

o   Usually like *u* in English *mud*, but rounder.

When final sound in word, and often before *s* and *z*, like ô.

ô   Approximately like *oa* in *coat*.

oe, oeu   Like *eu*.

oi   Approximately like a combination of the consonant *w* and the *a* of *calm*.

ou, oû,
où   Like *ou* in *tour*.

p   At end of words, usually silent.

Between *m* and *t*, *m* and *s*, *r* and *s*, usually silent.

Elsewhere, as in English.

pn, ps   Unlike English, when *pn* and *ps* occur at the beginning of words the *p* is usually sounded.

ph   Like *f*.

qu   Usually like *k*.

r   A vibration either of the uvula, or of the tip of the tongue against the upper front teeth.

See above under *er*.

s   Generally, like *s* in *sea*.

Single *s* between vowels, like *z* in *zone*.

At end of words, normally silent.

sc   Before *e* or *i*, like *s*.

Elsewhere, like *sk*.

t   Approximately like English *t*, but pronounced with tongue tip against teeth.

At end of words, normally silent.

When followed by *ie, ion, ium, ius,* and other diphthongs beginning with a vowel, *t* generally is like English *s* in sea (unless the *t* itself is preceded by an *s* or an *x*).

th   Like *t*.

u, û   A vowel sound not found in English; like

ue   After *c* or *g* and before *il*, like *eu*.

v   As in English.

w   Usually like *v*; in some people's pronunciation, like English *w*.

x   Generally sounds like *ks*; but when the syllable *ex* begins a word and is followed by a vowel, *x* sounds like *gz*.

At end of words, usually silent.

y   Generally like *i* in *machine*; but when between two vowels, like *y* in *yes*.

z   Like *z* in *zone*.

At end of words, often silent (see above under *ez*).

German Pronunciation Guide

CONSONANTS

b   Usually like English *b*: **Bett, graben.** But when final or before *s* or *t*, like English *p*: **das Grab, des Grabs, er gräbt.**

c   In foreign words only. Before *a, o, u,* like English *k*: **Café'.** Before *ä, e, i* in words borrowed from Latin, like English *ts*: **Cicero;** otherwise usually with the foreign pronunciation.

ch   After *a, o, u, au,* a scraping sound like Scottish *ch* in *loch,* made between the back of the tongue and the roof of the mouth: **Dach, Loch, Buch, auch.** In other positions, much like English *h* in *hue*: **Dächer, Löcher, Bücher, ich, manch, welch, durch.** In words borrowed from Greek or Latin, initial *ch* before *a, o, u, l, r* is like English *k*: **Charak'ter, Chor, Christ.** In words borrowed from French it is like German *sch*: **Chance.**

chs   As a fixed combination, like English *ks*: **der Dachs,** *the badger.* But when the *s* is an ending, like German *ch* plus *s*: **des Dachs,** genitive of **das Dach,** *the roof.*

ck As in English: **backen, Stock.**

d Usually like English *d:* **Ding, Rede.** But when final or before *s,* like English *t:* **das Band, des Bands.**

dt Like English *tt:* **Stadt** just like statt.

f As in English: **Feuer, Ofen, Schaf.**

g Usually like English *g* in *get:* **Geld, schlagen, Könige, reinigen.** But when final or before *s* or *t,* like English *k:* **der Schlag, des Schlags, er schlägt.** However, *ig* when final or before *s* or *t* is like German *ich:* **der König, des Königs, er reinigt.** In words borrowed from French, *g* before *e* is like English *z* in *azure:* **Loge.**

h As in English: **hier.** But after vowels it is only a sign of vowel length, and is not pronounced: **gehen, Bahn, Kuh.**

j Like English *y:* **Jahr.** In a few words borrowed from French, like English *z* in *azure:* **Journal'.**

k As in English: **kennen, Haken, buk.**

l Not the "dark *l*" of English *mill, bill,* but the "bright *l*" of English *million, billion:* **lang, fallen, hell.**

m As in English: **mehr, kommen, dumm.**

n As in English: **neu, kennen, kann.**

ng Always like English *ng* in *singer,* never like English *ng* + *g* in *finger.* **German Finger, Hunger.**

p As in English: **Post, Rippe, Tip.**

pf Like English *pf* in cupful: **Kopf, Apfel, Pfund.**

ph As in English: **Philosophie'.**

qu Like English *kv:* **Quelle, Aqua'rium.**

r When followed by a vowel, either a gargled sound made between the back of the tongue and the roof of the mouth, or (less commonly) a quick flip of the tongue tip against the gum ridge: **Ring, Haare, bessere.** When not followed by a vowel, a sound much like the *ah* of English *yeah,* or the *a* of *sofa:* **Haar, besser.**

s Usually like English *z* in *zebra,* or *s* in *rose:* **sie, Rose.** But when final or before a consonant, like English *s* in *this:* das, Wespe, **Liste, Maske.**

sch Like English *sh* in *ship,* but with the lips rounded: **Schiff, waschern, Tisch.**

sp ⎫ At the beginning of a word, like *sch* + *p,*
st ⎭ *sch* + *t:* **Spiel, Stahl.**

ss ⎫ Like English *ss* in *miss.* *ss* is written only
ß ⎭ after a short vowel when another vowel follows: **müssen.** Otherwise ß is written: finally **muß,** before a constant **muß**te, or

after a long vowel Muße.

t As in English: tun, bitter, Blatt.

th Always like *t:* Theater; never like English *th.*

tion Pronounced *tsyohn:* **Nation', Aktion'.**

tsch Like *t* + *sch:* **deutsch.**

tz Like English *ts:* **sitzen, Platz.**

v In German words, like English *f:* **Vater, Frevel.** In foreign words, like English *v:* **Novem'ber, Moti've;** but finally and before *s,* like *f* again: **das Motiv', des Motivs'.**

w Like English *v:* **Wagen, Löwe.**

x As in English: **Hexe.**

z Always like English *ts:* **zehn, Kreuz, Salz.**

SHORT VOWELS

a	Satz	Between English *o* in *hot* and *u* in *hut.*
ä	Sätze	⎫ Like English *e* in *set.*
e	setze	⎭
i	sitze	Like English *i* in *sit.*
o	Stock	Like English *o* in *gonna,* or the "New England short *o*" in *coat, road;* shorter than English *o* in *cost.*
ö	Stöcke	Tongue position as for short *e,* lips rounded as for short *o.*
u	Busch	Like English *u* in *bush.*
ü	Büsche	⎫ Tongue position as for short *i,*
y	mystisch	⎭ lips rounded as for short *u.*

UNACCENTED SHORT E

e beginne   Like English *e* in *begin, pocket.*

LONG VOWELS

a	Tal	⎫
ah	Zahl	⎬ Like English *a* in *father.*
aa	Saal	⎭
ä	Täler	⎫ In elevated speech, like English
äh	zählen	⎭ *ai* in *fair;* otherwise just like German long *e.*
e	wer	⎫ Like English *ey* in *they,* but with
eh	mehr	⎬ no glide toward a *y* sound.
ee	Meer	⎭
i	mir	⎫ Like English *i* in *machine,* but
ih	ihr	⎬ with no glide toward a *y*
ie	Bier	⎭ sound.

o	**Ton**	} Like English *ow* in *slow*, but with no glide toward a *w* sound.
oh	**Sohn**	
oo	**Boot**	

ö	**Töne**	} Tongue position as for long *e*, lips rounded as for long *o*.
öh	**Söhne**	
u	**Hut**	} Like English *u* in *rule*, but with no glide toward a *w* sound.
uh	**Kuh**	
ü	**Hüte**	} Tongue position as for long *i*, lips rounded as for long *u*.
üh	**Kühe**	
y	**Typ**	

DIPHTHONGS

ei	**Seite**	} Like English *i* in *side*. Also spelled *ey, ay* in names: *Meyer, Bayern*.
ai	**Saite**	
au	**Haut**	Like English *ou* in *out*.
eu	**heute**	} Like English *oi* in *oil*.
äu	**Häute**	

THE SPELLING OF VOWEL LENGTH

An accented vowel is always short when followed by a doubled consonant letter, but nearly always long when followed by a single consonant letter.

SHORT	LONG
schlaff	Schlaf
wenn	wen
still	Stil
offen	Ofen
öffnen	Öfen
Butter	Puter
dünne	Düne

Note that ck counts as the doubled form of k: tz counts as the doubled form of z:

hacken Haken
putzen duzen

GERMAN ACCENTUATION

Most German words are accented on the first syllable: **Mo'nate, ar'beitete, Düsenkampfflugzeuge.** However, the prefixes be-, emp-, ent-, er-, ge-, ver-, zer- are never accented: **befeh'len, der Befehl', empfan'gen, der Empfang'**, etc. Other prefixes are usually accented in nouns: **der Un'terricht,** but unaccented in verbs: **unterrich'ten.** Foreign words are often accented on a syllable other than the first: **Hotel', Muse'um, Photographie'.**

Note particularly the accentuation of such forms as **übertre'ten, ich übertre'te** *I overstep*, where **über** is a prefix; but **ü'bertreten, ich trete . . . über** *I step over* where **über** is a separate word, despite the fact that **ü'bertreten** is spelled without a space.

Italian Pronunciation Guide

ITALIAN LETTER	PRONUNCIATION
a	Like English *a* in *father*.
b	As in English.
c	Before *e* or *i*, and sometimes at the end of words, like English *ch*. Elsewhere, like English *k*.
ch	Before *e* or *i*, like English *k*.
ci	Before *a, o,* or *u*, like English *ch*.
d	As in English.
é	("close *e*") Like English *ay* in *day*, but with no final *y*-like glide.
è	("open *e*") Like English *e* in *bet*.
e	Like English *e* in *bet*.
f	As in English.
g	Before *e* or *i*, like English *g* in *gem*. Elsewhere, like English *g* in *go*.
gh	Before *e* or *i*, like English *g* in *go*.

gi	Before *a, o,* or *u*, like English *g* in *gem*.
gl	Before *i*, normally like English *lli* in *million*.
gli	Before *a, e, o,* or *u*, like English *lli* in *million*.
gn	Like English *ny* in *canyon*.
h	After *c* and *g*, indicates "hard" pronunciation of preceding consonant letter. Elsewhere, silent.
i	After *c, g,* and (normally) *sc*, before *a, o,* or *u*, indicates "soft" pronunciation of preceding consonant letter or letters. Elsewhere: When unstressed and before or after another vowel, like English *y*. Otherwise, like English *i* in *machine*, but with no final *y*-like glide.

j At the end of words, when replacing it in some noun plurals, like Italian *i*.

Otherwise, like English *y*.

k As in English.

l Like English *l* in *like*, but with the tongue behind the upper front teeth.

m As in English.

n As in English.

ó ("close *o*") Like English *o* in *go*, but with no final *w*-like glide

ò ("open *o*") Like English *o* in *bought*.

o Like English *o* in *bought*.

p As in English.

qu Like English *qu* in *quick*.

r Not at all like American English *r*; a quick flap of the tip of the tongue on the gumridge.

s Between vowels, like English *s* in *lease* (in southern Italy); like *s* in *please* (in northern Italy); sometimes like *s* in *lease* and sometimes like *s* in *please* (in central Italy).

Before *b, d, g, l, m, n, r, v*, like English *z*.

Elsewhere, like English *s* in *same, stick*.

sc Before *e* or *i*, and occasionally at the end of words, like English *sh*.

Elsewhere, like English *sk*.

sch Before *e* or *i*, like English *sk*.

sci Before *a, o,* or *u*, like English *sh*.

t As in English.

u When unstressed and before or after another vowel, like English *w*.

Otherwise, like English *oo* in *boot*, but without final *w*-like glide.

v As in English.

w Rare; like English *v*.

x Rare; like English *x*.

z Like English *ts* in *cats* or like English *dz* in *adze*.

CONSONANT LENGTH

All Italian consonants occur both single (short) and double (long); in the latter instance, the time of their pronunciation lasts from one-and-a-half to two times that of the single consonants.

ITALIAN ACCENTUATION

In most conventional writing and printing, spoken stress is marked by a grave accent (` ` `), but only when it falls on the last syllable of a word: *città, vendè, lunedì, cantò, tribù*. An accent is placed over the vowel letter of some words to distinguish them from others having the same spelling and pronunciation but differing in meaning: *è* "is" versus *e* "and." In other instances, stress is usually left unmarked, although it may fall on any syllable up to the sixth from the end.